BEAUTIFULLY BROKEN

Healing From Shame And Brokenness

TRACI SMITH

Beautifully Broken
Healing From Shame And Brokenness
By Traci Smith

Printed in the United States of America

ISBN 9781498423526

www.xulonpress.com

DEDICATION

For the broken and shamed. You are beautiful.

ACKNOWLEDGEMENTS

*Thank you to my husband, children, family, and friends
who learned to love me no matter what, and, most of all,
to my Heavenly Father who loved me all along.*

TABLE OF CONTENTS

PREFACE

Three years ago, I made a sinful choice with my body that led to the end of a sixteen-year marriage. I am a pastor's wife who committed adultery. Although my affair only lasted two months, it easily smashed our family to pieces. Since that time, the Lord has lovingly and mercifully led me down a road to restoration—a road, not just for me, but for other shamed and broken women.

Beautifully Broken is my restoration journey from adultery to purity. If you are reading this preface with ANY sense of shame or brokenness because of sin in your life (sexual or otherwise), the Lord wants you to know that you are NOT "too far gone." You CAN return. You CAN start over.

My hope and prayer for you, *Beautifully Broken One*, is that you will be restored through my personal story. During my season of brokenness, the Lord revealed to me "Seven Steps to Restoration" that you may find helpful in your own journey back. I believe these steps, coupled with honest and often raw testimony, will be just the "resin" you need to "piece" your life back together.

Each chapter ends with "Reflections at the Well" which contains questions and action steps for personal reflection to be shared with a counselor, accountability partner, small group, or class. This "homework" time is necessary "heart work" time essential to your restoration and healing. Think of it as your "backpack" of blessings on your journey back.

Just like the Samaritan woman, we all shamefully walk that road to the well in hope that, in spite of our brokenness, we can still be filled to the rim with living water (John 4:7).

I am humbled to walk this restoration road with you. It is my sincere prayer that you will find what you are looking for. He stands ready to take your broken jar, seam it back together with gold resin, and fill it to over-flowing with living water. Drink and never be thirsty again.

Beautifully Broken,

Traci

Introduction

MY ADULTEROUS FIX

"How did I get here?" I whispered. My sweaty palms had a "death grip" on the steering wheel as I once again made the long drive down that all-too-familiar road. Like all the times before, I found myself short of breath, anticipating the day ahead while suffocating under the weight of my shame. It was as if I was drowning, and I was clinging to the steering wheel to save me.

The once-beautiful Texas wildflowers now glowed like colorful traffic cones in the early morning sun. "Where are you going, Traci?" they cautioned. "Turn back before it is too late!"

It was already too late. I was now an addict, and this addict needed another "fix."

HE was my drug— an "injection of escape" from the mundane of my life, a drug that sent thrills through my body with every text, every word, and every touch. He said all the "right" things and hauntingly seemed to know me better than I knew myself. The "highs" from a "hit" with him always left me wanting more.

And so I drove. I drove to escape. But, most of all, I drove to forget.

I wanted to forget the pain of my reality—broken people with broken promises based on unattainable false loves of performance and perfection. A Christian pastor's wife, doting mother of three boys, and successful business woman, I hid my dirty little secret from everyone.

The truth was, *I was living a double life.* Underneath my perfect façade of neatly pressed Sunday blouses were the painful scars of a Scarlet Letter "A." I was having an affair with another man—an affair that began on Facebook.

A modern-day woman fed by reality shows and trash TV, I began to believe the relentless lie the entertainment industry sold me that life was ALWAYS "greener" on the other side. I longed for the excitement that came from someone seducing me the way men seduced women on soap operas.

So, when I innocently wished a former high school acquaintance "Happy Birthday" through a haphazard Facebook post, and he responded with what I believed was a "sincere" compliment, I saw it as my "open gate" to greener pastures.

That now infamous "birthday" post quickly led to private messages, to the exchange of phone numbers, to hidden texting, to dirty sexting, to a sexual encounter face-to-face on my way home from work. I can remember thinking to myself, "Did that REALLY happen?" as I shamefully fled the scene of the crime. I justified my "slip" as a "one time thing," telling myself that it would never happen again. But it did.

The line of morality that once clearly separated reality from fantasy became more and more blurred with each raunchy rendezvous. He told me he loved me, and I believed him.

The truth was, it was not a love story at all. I was a pawn in his deceptive game. My "true love," in reality, was a dangerous sexual predator who had to be escorted in and out of Texas courthouses by armed guards. He had threatened to kill a judge and an attorney, and now he planned to "kill" my marriage.

When I was scoping out greener pastures on Facebook, he was scoping out candidates to play the role of wife and mother in a desperate act to gain custody of his three young daughters.

In my most "stoned" state, I could easily overlook his alcoholism, abuse, and unhealthy obsession with a woman's body. With him, I could be myself—no expectations. I did not have to try to be perfect to please the church crowd because to him, "I was perfect."

His charming tactics became the fuel that ran every road trip. As my car neared the city limits of his small rural town, my mind replayed our meetings before like a thrilling pornographic movie masked as a true love story. I could not wait for him to touch me again. He loved my flawed body; and I loved him for that.

The garage door of his two-story home was left open for me on days I would visit. Small town people talk, and since he was running for public office, his reputation was of utmost importance. Paranoid that someone was always watching him, he made sure that the door closed immediately behind me before revealing himself.

He kept me tucked away and hidden, all to himself. We rarely left the home, mostly to keep me from learning the truth. The truth was he was a lie.

Although he "pushed" himself to me as a self-made, vineyard-owning millionaire, in reality, he was broke. In an effort to win potential bonus points at his upcoming custody hearing, he created a fake church website on which he sold himself as an ordained minister. In reality, he was a professed atheist.

These truths, which would later come to the surface, were masked by the man he wanted me to see.

His worn face, thin physique, and slicked hair reminded me of the Marlboro man—rugged and mysterious but with an artistic flair. He wore a tacky Hawaiian button up, faded blue jeans, and flip flops. His kisses were laced with cigarette smoke.

"Come with me," he said as he led me by the hand to the front room of his house. It was a particularly pleasant spring day, so the window shades were pulled aside to reveal wide open windows. "Here?" I asked. "But your neighbor will see us."

"Who cares," he snickered back. "Maybe he will learn a thing or two."

I was not surprised at his exhibitionist antics. You see, in his dark world, the more "out there" it was, the better. He was an uninhibited artist, and to him, the most beautiful canvas was a woman's body. He studied my body, like an artist studies his muse. Then, when he was fully inspired, he would use his hands to paint me into his latest masterpiece.

We would spend the day in each other's arms, debating topics that he knew would challenge me. He would try his best to convince me that God did not exist, and I would try my best to convince him that he did.

The brainwashing was subtle, but over time, I became more and more confused. I did not know what I believed anymore. As I became less and less of me, I became more and more of what he wanted me to be. I wanted to please him more than anyone else.

Our lively debates often led to scary and dark places. When massive amounts of alcohol and cigarettes were added to the mix, he became a very dangerous and abusive cocktail. In drunken fits of rage, he would demand that I divorce my husband and marry him. And when I refused, he called me a coward.

His utter disgust with me led to moments of deep depression and suicidal thoughts, which he only encouraged by handing me a loaded gun. If he did not care if I lived or died, who would?

My addict "highs" were met with the lowest of "lows" as I would experience withdrawals from my drug each time we parted ways. We would say our "good-byes" as we said our "hellos"—in secret.

As I hurried back on to that all-too-familiar road with the imprint of his scent still fresh on my body, I would sneak back to my reality with the same unspoken fear that, this time, I would get caught.

And this time, I did...

Section One:

CRACKS

Chapter 1

DIRTY LITTLE SECRETS

Now the serpent was more crafty than any of the wild animals the Lord
God had made. He said to the woman, "Did God really say,
'You must not eat from any tree in the garden?"
(Genesis 3:1)

Kintsugi is the Japanese art form of taking "perfectly good" pottery, breaking it, and then piecing it back together with seams of gold. In doing so, the pottery becomes more valuable. Its beauty is in its brokenness.

Many of us could compare our Christian journey to the art of kintsugi. Just like that "perfectly good" pottery, we are often shattered to pieces through a sinful struggle between good and evil. "For our struggle is not against flesh and blood, but against the rulers, against the authorities, against the powers of this dark world and against the spiritual forces of evil in the heavenly realms" (Philippians 1:12).

Satan and his demonic team of "thugs" continually study our weak areas, and just when we let down our guard, they strike—what was once an "innocent mistake" instantaneously becomes a deliberate destructive pattern. The slippery slope of sin causes us to lose a grip on our reality. Before we realize it, we are spiraling out of control to the rock hard surfaces below. What was once beautiful is now broken.

I was once "perfectly good" pottery. Created by the Creator from a single lump of clay, I was molded from the beginning by the hands of a mom and dad cursed by generational sin. Cracked by the shame of childhood sexual abuse and the non-stop pressures of performance and perfection, I was doomed from the beginning. These hidden cracks would fragile my faith, allowing Satan to seep in to my life and ultimately break me through the sin of adultery.

I grew up in a "Christian" home with a dad who was a "workaholic," a mom who was a "perfectionist" and an older sister, who in my eyes was always the "favorite." Early on, I grew to believe that love was conditional—based on performance and perfection. As long as I performed for my dad and looked absolutely perfect for my mom, I could *almost* be the "favorite." "Almost" being the key word.

CRACKED BY THE SHAME OF CHILDHOOD SEXUAL ABUSE AND THE NON-STOP PRESSURES OF PERFOR-MANCE AND PERFECTION, I WAS DOOMED FROM THE BEGINNING.

The truth was, I could never be good enough. My earliest memories of "perfection" pressures are from my preschool years. I can remember crying outside my bedroom door when friends came over to play, terrified of my mom finding my room in less-than-perfect condition. NOTHING could be out of place, including my appearance from head to toe—beautifully bound hair buns, perfectly pressed dresses, matching purses, and matching shoes. Flawless perfection was the goal.

As for my dad, he was not around much due to work commitments. Although he had earned Master's degrees from two Ivy-league universities, he had turned down promising career opportunities to take over our 100-year old plus family business—partly out of guilt, but mostly out of obligation. He was the oldest of three sons, and it really was not an option.

My dad's dad, his namesake, was a stern business man who rarely broke a smile. He worked long hours to please his dad who had worked long hours to please his dad before him. Work proved your worth in their family, and they all ran the "performance wheel" like it was nobody's business. It was a senseless cycle of people pleasing, passed down from generation to generation. Love was absolutely conditional—based on your performance. And your performance had better be perfect.

Sadly, not one dad ever told his son, "I love you," because no one ever did enough to earn it.

I believe it was this sense of guilt and obligation, driven by a profound lack of "I love you," that literally drove my dad to work all the time. It was as if he was trying to prove something to someone. Maybe it was to prove that he was worthy of love. Deep down inside, he just wanted to please his dad—a character trait that he passed to me.

The only difference is that I never questioned my dad's love for me. He always made sure he told me, "I love you"—almost to a fault.

I often laugh that my parents had two daughters, and I was the "son" they never had. I was, and still am, a "tom boy" at heart. Because my older sister was naturally more "girly" than me, she seemed, in my eyes, to be my mom's "favorite." So, I tried desperately to be my dad's—"daddy's little girl."

No amount of perfection or performance could cover the hidden shame I carried deep within—the biggest "crack" of them all. Tucked tightly behind my earned titles of "perfect daughter" and "daddy's little girl," was a title I gave myself. "Daddy's little girl" was a "dirty little girl." I was a victim of childhood sexual abuse.

My childhood years were plagued with secret episodes of cutting, self-inflicted pain, anxiety, depression, sweaty palms, and wetting myself—all manifestations of childhood sexual abuse. For some reason, the Lord has spared me from remembering all the abusive details. To this day, I can only recall an instance or two that could be viewed as "inappropriate." What I do remember, very clearly, is feeling shame.

Performance. Perfection. Abuse. These cracks in my early "moldable" years created strongholds in my life that fashioned me into a "perfectly good" piece of pottery.

> TO THIS DAY, I CAN ONLY RECALL AN INSTANCE OR TWO THAT COULD BE VIEWED AS "INAPPROPRIATE." WHAT I DO REMEMBER, VERY CLEARLY, IS FEELING SHAME.

Strongholds

This is how the generational sin of adultery is birthed. The roots of performance, perfection and childhood sexual abuse grow a "trunk," like adultery, that produces an abundance of "rotten fruit" later in life like shame, depression, anxiety and low self-esteem. Before we know it, these "rotten fruits" become strongholds in a believer's life.

A stronghold, as defined by Liberty Savard in her book titled *Shattering Your Strongholds*, is "Anything you rely upon to fortify, defend, and protect your personal beliefs, whether they are right or wrong."

According to Savard, the typical pattern of sin is as follows:

1. Something *traumatic* happens in my life which is ***a fact***

2. which leads me to develop *a wrong pattern of thinking*

3. which helps me justify *a wrong behavior*

4. which causes me to erect *a stronghold* to protect my right do so

5. *which perpetuates my pain by keeping the trauma locked in and God locked out.*

In my situation as a child...

1. I was sexually abused [*a traumatic event, a fact*].
2. which led me to think that sex outside of marriage was acceptable [*a wrong pattern of thinking*].
3. which justified my adulterous act [*a wrong behavior*]
4. which caused me to erect a stronghold of shame [*a stronghold*]
5. which perpetuated my pain through hiding the truth—ultimately locking Satan's lie in and locking God's truth out. [*perpetuated pain*]

This process that develops a pattern (and habit) of sin has been around since the creation of the world. Just look at Adam, Eve, and the serpent in the Garden of Eden.

The Lord God took the man and put him in the Garden of Eden to work it and take care of it. And the Lord God commanded the man, "You are free to eat from any tree in the garden; but you must not eat from the tree of the knowledge of good and evil, for when you eat of it you will surely die." (Genesis 2:15-17)

Short, sweet, and to the point, the Lord makes the boundary of sin very clear to Adam. But in Genesis Chapter 3, the serpent, let's call him "Mr. Sneaky Snake," twists the truth, and himself, into the shape of a question mark, asking Eve the most clever of clarifications, "Did God really say...?"

And with that simple phrase, "Did God really say...?" God's period became a question mark. That question mark opens up the door to habitual sin that may be passed on generationally until the curse is broken.

Connecting-the-Dots in My Childhood

As I have worked relentlessly since my affair to peel away the "reasons why" I committed adultery, Satan has caused me to question everything about my past, especially what happened to me as a child.

"Did someone really sexually abuse you?" Satan slithers a question mark over a fact. "You are just making this whole thing up for attention. You are a liar, Traci. You are the one who is dirty!"

Looking back, the signs of abuse were all there, lined up in a not-so pretty little picture of a sin-laced Connect-the-Dots.

During my preschool years, I spent much of my time alone. When my mom would discover me missing for long periods of time, she would often find me alone in my room.

"Whatcha doing in here alone, Traci?" she would ask.

"DID SOMEONE REALLY SEXUALLY ABUSE YOU?" SATAN SLITHERS A QUESTION MARK OVER A FACT. "YOU ARE JUST MAKING THIS WHOLE THING UP FOR ATTENTION. YOU ARE A LIAR, TRACI. YOU ARE THE ONE WHO IS DIRTY!"

"I am being lonely," I answered back in a matter-of-fact way.

For some reason, I preferred being alone. It felt safe. No one could make me feel "less than," and I did not have to please anyone.

In the secret of my room, I would act out mini soap operas with my stuffed animals and Barbie dolls playing the lead rolls. I would erect temporary walls to their pretend houses using the sleeves of my favorite records. In those rooms, I would play "house." The dolls were always naked, and there was always kissing, touching, and sex.

When I grew bored of the limitations of my make-believe, plastic characters, I began experimenting with my peers in a game we called "house."

I would undress and encourage my girlfriends to do the same. We would snuggle under the covers of my twin bed.

I will never forget the time I got caught. My mom had peeked her head in the room to check on me, just as she had done so many times before, only to find me curled up in covers and flush-faced on the edge of my bed. My friend hid under the covers. I felt so ashamed.

"Please do not tell Dad," I pled fearfully in tears. "Please do not tell Dad!"

For some reason, I was more concerned about my father's disappointment than anyone else's. Deep down, I was afraid of not being his "favorite" anymore—a title I had worked hard to earn.

"Get dressed you two," she said with disgust and closed the door behind her. Nothing else was ever said about that incident, but in my childlike thinking, my mom never looked at me the same.

As time went on, these incidences became "my dirty little secrets." My abuse began to manifest itself physically. When I would laugh just a little too much, as I would often do, I would feel a warm stream of stinging urine trickle down my leg.

I would wet myself often, and shamefully in the most public of places. If I thought it was noticeable, I would hide my soiled shorts with a tied t-shirt around my waist. Sometimes I would sit for hours in wet clothing just to avoid someone finding out. I went through clothes like they were almost disposable.

Social situations, as simple as preschool and elementary school, were awkward and uncomfortable. Because my first and last name initials were "TT" I was an obvious target for name-calling (they had no idea how on point the nickname "Tee Tee" really was). I wore ugly leg braces from waist to feet and spoke with a speech impediment, both only added to the already brutal teasing. Anxiety attacks were so severe that I could hardly catch my breath as we neared the school drop off line, and my palms were always dripping with sweat.

To numb out from the shame and pain I felt on an almost constant basis, I began purposefully hurting myself. Late at night, in the secret of my room, I would lay flat on my back in my "dirty" little bed, banging my head back against the hard, green, fence-shaped headboard over and over again.

"YOU ARE A BAD LITTLE GIRL," I WOULD SCOLD MYSELF, "A BAD LITTLE GIRL."

"You are a bad little girl," I would scold myself, "a bad little girl."

In some strange way, hurting myself gave me a sense of control and helped to alleviate some of the guilt I felt. I wanted to punish myself, because in my warped sense of worth, what happened to me was my fault.

Even at a very young age, I hated my body. I felt repulsed, dirty, and most of all shamed by what I saw in the mirror. No amount of hair-sprayed buns, pretty ruffled dresses or shiny red shoes could make me feel any less of an "ugly duckling."

Underneath it all, I hid my "dirty little secrets" from everyone, and I shamefully carried them with me everywhere I went.

No one could ever find out. As far as I was concerned, no one ever would.

Reflections at the Well

According to Liberty Savard, "What is a stronghold?"

Given the "typical pattern of sin," as well as my own example, prayerfully ask the Lord to reveal to you your own "pattern" of sin. Write this pattern below:

Something traumatic happens in my life: _____-> which leads me to develop a wrong pattern of thinking: _____-> which helps me justify a wrong behavior: _____-> which causes me to erect a stronghold to protect my right to do so: _____-> which perpetuates my pain by keeping the trauma locked in and God locked out.

What does God's Word say about "the weapons of our warfare" (2 Corinthians 10:4-5) and how does this give you hope?

End your time at the Well by asking the Lord, through prayer, to continue to reveal any strongholds in your life that must be exposed for your complete restoration and healing. Thank Him for His mighty weapons of warfare that will pull down your strongholds, giving you the ultimate victory for His glory.

Chapter 2

STAINED BY SHAME

Those who look to him are radiant, their faces are never covered with shame.
(Psalm 34:5)

There is a quaint little coffee shop in my hometown, aptly named "Mugwalls," in which the walls of the shop are literally decorated with a "hodge podge" of stained coffee mugs donated by those who frequent the shop.

Mugwalls is where all the Christian college kids tend to hang out, mainly because of its Christian ownership, proximity to the Texas A&M University campus, and the nearby offices of a popular college Bible study called "Breakaway."

I like to come here to write. In fact, as I write this chapter, I am literally sitting in my favorite rickety chair at my favorite wobbly table near the entrance of the shop. One by one, the faces of people I do not know with stories I have never heard, enter the shop through its squeaky front door.

They grab their favorite "cup of Joe," often poured in a mug brought from home, drop down on one of the cushy thrift shop couches and sleep, socialize, or dare I say—study. And when the time comes to face the "real" world outside these fragrant walls, patrons either take their mug with them or leave it for someone else's enjoyment in the future.

I cannot help but wonder about the stories behind the discarded coffee mugs. How many of them bear the invisible cracks of a shameful secret? How many are really broken?

Recently, as I was sharing my possible plans to write this very book with a friend of mine just outside the shop, a young woman approached our courtyard table.

"Excuse me," she said. "I could not help but over hear your plans to write a book. Would you mind telling me more about it?"

As I began to explain my shameful past and God's call on my life to write this book, she interrupted.

"I have a shameful past," she exclaimed with tears in her eyes.

She went on to explain that even though she grew up in a Christian home, she was sexually active during her high school and college years.

"I was so ashamed by my actions that I literally stopped attending my church. When I finally mustered up the courage to go back, I was shamed all over again by a woman who was my mentor."

"Where have you been?" her "Christian" mentor asked when she discovered her sitting on the back row of the sanctuary. "Is everything okay?"

"I explained my shameful actions to her, and how I felt like I could not show my face at church because of them."

"Wow! That is understandable," she replied, followed by a judgmental whisper. "That really IS shameful."

Cracks Created by Shame

As I listened to this young recent college graduate recount her mentor's hurtful words, I could not help but think back to my own promiscuous high school and college years. I, too, felt shamed by the choices I made with my body.

In that season of my life, I was unaware of the "cracks" created in my own stained "mug" by a *shameful* past of childhood sexual abuse. These "cracks" would eventually break me, and my life, to pieces.

Up until high school, I viewed anything sexual as shameful and dirty. Sex was simply not discussed in our home. The thought of boys touching me made me cringe. My childhood nickname of "Tee Tee" evolved in to a new nickname, "Double Tease" because I always flirted with the boys but never "put out." I liked the attention, but felt a sense of rejection and shame each time they called me out by the name they had given me.

I WAS UNAWARE OF THE "CRACKS" CREATED IN MY OWN STAINED "MUG" BY A SHAMEFUL PAST OF CHILDHOOD SEXUAL ABUSE.

It was not until my senior year in high school that I really started experimenting sexually, partly out of curiosity, but mostly out of peer pressure.

I was tired of the teasing, and because I had grown up running the "performance wheel" like nobody's business, I would do anything to please people, especially the high school boys. Maybe if I performed enough for them, I could be "their favorite" and the teasing would stop. Kissing turned in to touching turned in to oral sex, and ultimately, the shame of sexual sin.

I carried the "dirtiness" of sexual shame to college, joining the same sorority as my sister. But unlike my sister, I felt most comfortable around the "bad" girls. I did everything to fit in, including drinking alcohol, smoking cigarettes, and eventually having sex.

I can still remember my "first time." My "sisters" and I had attended a mixer with a local fraternity, at which I had enjoyed more than my fair share of "flaming Dr. Peppers." Because I was drunk and in no condition to drive, one of the "frat" boys generously offered to give me a ride home. This "innocent" ride home turned shameful when I found myself naked in his top bunk, his body forcefully pressed upon mine.

"Stop," I whispered. "Please stop!"

Although I pled and pushed my captor away, he did not stop. Shamefully, my virginity was stolen that night when I was raped by my "innocent" ride home. The next morning, I woke up with a serious hangover in a bed that was not my own.

The feeling was all too familiar. Once again, I was naked and ashamed. With his blood-stained sheets tucked tightly in my arms, I walked in complete humiliation from his apartment to my dorm room to try to wash away the dirtiness. The stains of shame may have come out of those sheets, but they did not come out of my soul until years later.

SHAMEFULLY, MY VIRGINITY WAS STOLEN THAT NIGHT WHEN I WAS RAPED BY MY "INNOCENT" RIDE HOME.

That is the way shame works. It stains you. From the moment that Satan threw that question mark over God's command, "You are free to eat from any tree in the garden; but you must not eat from the tree of the knowledge of good and evil" (Genesis 2:16-17), Adam and Eve were "set up" for the stain of sin. It was almost a "sure thing."

It is like the telephone game. As the original message, or command in this case, is passed from person to person, the message somehow is morphed into something that was never intended at all. Shame was never God's intention.

When asked, "Did God really say?" (Genesis 3:1) the woman (that is right, blame it on "the woman") tweaked the message ever so slightly in a biblical version of the telephone game.

"We may eat fruit from the trees in the garden, but God did say, 'You must not eat fruit from the tree that is in the middle of the garden, and you must not touch it, or you will die" (Genesis 3:2-3).

I am sorry—I thought he said, "eat" and not "touch." In any case, we all know what happened next. They bit the bait—hook, line, and sinker. When they did, shame became the original sin. You can almost see Satan taking a swig of satisfaction from his favorite can of soda, labeled "Shame," and then smiling from ear to sinister ear while humming the melody of "Can't Beat the Real Thing" under his breath.

In shame, Adam and Eve covered themselves. "Then the eyes of both of them were opened, and they realized they were naked. So they sewed fig leaves together and made covering for themselves" (Genesis 3:7). They covered themselves.

How are you "covering" your shame? Are you covering it with a Coke and a smile?

What comes next is quite ironic (as my best friend in high school used to say, "Irony can be pretty ironic sometimes"). The God of the Universe who knows all and sees all, asks our "happy" couple, "Where are you?" (Genesis 3:9). Really? Come on! You know very well where they are.

Call me a hopeless romantic, but I believe the Lord asks this question out of genuine, sincere love. It was as if he was saying, "I am still here and I love you just the same."

Just like me, they did not get it. "I heard you in the garden, and I was afraid (or insert "shamed") because I was naked; so I hid." How many of us, who have a history of sexual sin, hide? You know what I am talking about—we either "check out" from our family, church, Bible studies, and

Christian social circles, OR we "check out" from the reality of our sin in general.

The Lord, in His righteous anger and unconditional love, says, "Who told you that you were naked?" Who told you that you were too dirty to be deemed My child? Who told you that you were too stained to be saved? Who told you that you were too used to be used by Me?

Once word got out about me "putting out," I was passed from fraternity boy to fraternity boy, used and rejected each time in my quest to perform and be the "favorite." I bit the bait of shame—hook, line, and well, you know. From the outside, I looked healthy and whole, but inside I was secretly becoming more and more enslaved by my hidden sexual sin.

FROM THE OUTSIDE, I LOOKED HEALTHY AND WHOLE, BUT INSIDE, I WAS SECRETLY BECOMING MORE AND MORE ENSLAVED BY MY HIDDEN SEXUAL SIN.

The Toxic Soul Wounds of Sexual Sin

The soul wounds of sexual sin are toxic. Like an incurable disease, shame trickled over in to every area of my life. Not only was I failing out of school, but I was financially, emotionally, and spiritually bankrupt: *shame, shame, and more shame.* Because I believed the lie that Satan whispered in my ear over and over again, that I was "too broken" to be pieced back together, I slipped in to a deep depression, contemplating suicide on an almost daily basis.

I thought and felt that I was worthless—a used-up piece of filthy trash incapable of being loved. But God, in His infinite grace and mercy, was whispering, "Who told you that?" all along. Perhaps you have felt that

33

way, or are feeling that way right now. Circle the thoughts or feelings that you are experiencing at this very moment:

Shameful	Hate myself and my actions	Depressed		Worthless	Hopeless
Guilty	Desperate	Dirty	Cracked	Broken	Shattered

Other: _____

In October of that same freshman year, my sister invited me to attend Breakaway, the Bible study I mentioned at the beginning of this chapter, which met at a local middle school. Ironically, the Lord used that invitation from my sister, the one who I had always thought to be everyone's "favorite," to remind me that I was forever HIS favorite. In my most broken state, He reminded me of His message to His most broken of disciples, Paul:

> *Therefore, in order to keep me from becoming conceited, I was given a thorn in my flesh, a messenger of Satan, to torment me. Three times I pleaded with the Lord to take it away from me. But he said to me, 'My grace is sufficient for you, for my power is made perfect in weakness.' Therefore I will boast all the more gladly about my weaknesses, so that Christ's power may rest on me. That is why, for Christ's sake, I delight in weaknesses, in insults, in hardships, in persecutions, in difficulties. For when I am weak, then I am strong.* (2 Corinthians 12:7-10)

With that Scripture, God literally "broke in" to my heart.

How could a God so great know me so intimately?

It was on that night, on that very school library floor, that I surrendered my life to the true Lover of my Soul, Jesus Christ. Little did I know, that from that moment on, my life's calling and purpose would be to glorify

Him through the deep-rooted thorns in my flesh of sexual sin and brokenness. I was to be weak, so that He could be strong.

Sadly, my weakest moment was yet to come.

Reflections at the Well

How are you stained and shamed?

In what ways are you "covering" your shame?

What does 2 Corinthians 12:7-10 reveal to you about your "weaknesses?"

End your time at the Well by asking the Lord, through prayer, to give you the courage to no longer "cover" your shame, but rather to be brave enough to share it with others. Tell the Lord that you know His power is made perfect in your weaknesses, and that you will "boast all the more gladly about your weaknesses" so that His power may rest on you.

Chapter 3

THE FISH BOWL EFFECT

The Lord does not look at the things people look at. People look at the out-
ward appearance, but the Lord looks at the heart. (1 Samuel 16:7)

T he *Fish Bowl Effect*—it is a phenomenon they do not dare mention
in the course called "The Real Truth about Marriage in the Ministry
101." In fact, I do not believe they even offer such a course in seminary.
They should.

Based on a recent conversation with a friend of mine (a fellow pastor's wife with an adulterous past of her own), and our conversations with
other pastors' wives, we have coined our own "ministry" definition of this
phenomenon. The *Fish Bowl Effect* is the unspoken expectation of perfection unwillingly forced on pastors, their wives, and their children.

"It is about people looking at you and your family ALL the time,
having expectations ABOUT you and FOR you," my friend described.
"That is something they do not prepare you for in ministry!"

Amen, sister. Preach it!

Not to dwell on the subject of coffee mugs (an homage to Chapter 2),
but I have a favorite coffee mug at home that I pull out on those "special"

days. "Special" meaning, "Oh Lord, help me" kind of days. One could say, it keeps me "grounded" (no pun intended).

The mug's message is simple yet profound, "I Don't Remember Signing Up for This!"

Boy, if I had a dollar for every time I have thought THAT in our almost twenty years of marriage in the ministry! I would be, well, you know, rich.

I guess you could say that, on some subconscious level, I was trying to compensate for my own lack of "perfection" when I started dating my husband, Brian.

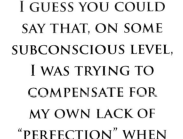

We met at Breakaway Bible study (the same Bible study I met the Lord at in the previous chapter) in the autumn of 1992 when we were introduced through a mutual friend—who just happened to be his ex-girlfriend. I can remember thinking, "This guy is really cute," but kept a healthy distance as his ex, one of my closest girlfriends, was still head over heels for him, and by the way, more "perfect" than me.

I GUESS YOU COULD SAY THAT, ON SOME SUBCONSCIOUS LEVEL, I WAS TRYING TO COMPENSATE FOR MY OWN LACK OF "PERFECTION" WHEN I STARTED DATING MY HUSBAND, BRIAN.

To me, he fit the stereotypical, preppy "Christian" mold. He looked Bible smart in his nerdy glasses and, no doubt, dressed to impress the "chicks" with his Polo sweaters, dry-cleaned khakis, and penny loafers. What a hunk!

We did not start dating until the following summer after bumping in to each other on campus during summer school. He asked me if I was going to be in College Station all summer, and when I said, "Yes," he suggested that we hang out sometime.

"Sometime" meant the very next day. That night, Brian, along with a "decoy" friend (who happened to be a girl), bravely showed up at my summer job—a well-known chain lingerie store, to ask for my phone number. To this day, we still laugh at my flirtatious response, "776-MENS." He called me the very next day to ask me out on our first date—dinner at the local Olive Garden followed by, arguably the worst first-date movie ever, "A River Runs Through It" (insert snoring sound here).

As we slurped our spaghetti and binged on never-ending baskets of breadsticks (talk about carb-loading), hours passed by like minutes. By the end of dinner, I knew that I was going to marry him, and he knew that he was going to marry me.

Married to the Ministry

Six months later, we were engaged, and thirteen months after that, we were married. As they say in the South, "Slam, bam, thank you, ma'am!"

I have to say that our marriage created quite the stir. High school friends were shocked that I was marrying a "pastor," given my untamed teen years. My sorority sisters were less than impressed. Of course, my parents were pleased as punch that such a "perfect" man had chosen their less-than-perfect daughter.

THERE WAS HOPE FOR ME YET, AS LONG AS I COULD PERFORM THE ROLE OF A "PERFECT" PASTOR'S WIFE.

There was hope for me yet, as long as I could perform the role of a "perfect" pastor's wife.

To be honest, I had some doubts about playing that role. I was, and still am, far from "perfect." Satan continued to remind me of my history of sexual sin. Beneath my perfectly polished "pastor's wife" exterior were the shameful scars of a Scarlett Letter A that continued to sting.

The irony of it all was that the Lord knew my history. In fact, the Lord knew me before my beginning. "For you created my inmost being; you knit me together in my mother's womb" (Psalm 137:13). This passage (oddly enough written by the adulterous David who carried his own weight of shame and regret) goes on to say that all our days were already planned out for us. The truth is this: the Lord knows our hurts, hang ups and habits, and He loves us just the same.

Sadly, like most believers, I did not get that until much later in life.

The Samaritan Woman—I Get Her

I dig the Samaritan woman at the well. In my own shameful way, I get her. Picture this, a woman who was so shamed by her own sexual sin that she waited until night fall, when no one else was around, to fetch her daily dose of water from the well. Talk about your hurts, hang ups, and habits! This woman was so hurt and hung up on her own sinful habits that she literally hid.

She, too, was far from "perfect," suffering from her own serious case of The Fishbowl Effect.

Yet Jesus met her imperfect self at the well anyway. I can only imagine her lipstick-stained stunned look when Jesus actually spoke to her, "Will you give me a drink?" (John 4:7).

"Is this guy serious?" she probably asked herself. "Does he realize who he's talking to? I am a _____ (insert your own shameful label here)."

Her answer back is so typical of someone caught in the death grips of shame. "You are a Jew and I am a Samaritan woman. How can you ask me for a drink?" (John 4:9). In parentheses, the Bible explains this was "because Jews did not associate with Samaritans." My shame-filled woman's intuition tells me differently. "Really? Is this all this guy wants from me? He does not want my body, but a drink instead?"

Trust is a huge issue for people who are shamed by sexual sin. Deep down inside, I believe the Samaritan woman did not trust Jesus' intentions. Deeper than that, she was ashamed of her own Scarlet Letter "A."

But aren't we all? What is YOUR Scarlet Letter "A"?

Church people, it is time for a little brutal, in-your-face honesty. We are ALL messy. We ALL have messes. Maybe your mess is not a Scarlett Letter A, but it is something. As we say in my family, "It is not *nothing*. It is definitely *something*." You are hiding something in the hopes that no one, especially your Christian circle of influence, will realize that you, dare I even say the words, are NOT "perfect."

God knows you are not "perfect." If you were perfect, the cross would have been unnecessary. We state the obvious to an all-knowing God, "I have no husband," the Samaritan woman said. Jesus said to her, "You are right when you say you have no husband. The fact is, you have had five husbands, and the man you now have is not your husband. What you have just said is quite true" (John 4:17-18).

SECRETS KEEP US SHAMED. BUT THE TRUTH, OUR OWN TRUTH ABOUT OUR MESSES AND THE TRUTH THAT IS JESUS, SETS US FREE.

But because Jesus knew it all and loved her anyway, many would come to know Christ through her. "Many of the Samaritans from that town believed in him because of the woman's testimony, 'He told me everything I ever did'" (John 4:39). I would add, "And, he loved me anyway."

Wouldn't it be great if, as believers in the same Jesus who loved the Samaritan woman sin and all, we offered the same grace and unconditional love that He modeled for us. "They overcame him (the Father of Lies) by the blood of the Lamb and by the word of their testimony" (Revelation 12:11). Secrets keep us shamed. But the truth, our own truth about our messes and the truth that is Jesus, sets us free (John 8:32).

Is Hiding Sin Possible?

What if we dared to share the truth about who we really are (our hurts, hang ups, and habits)? What if we used our messes as our message? What if we actually lived out a Culture of Redemption?

The purpose of *The Ultimate Journey* (a Bible study curriculum offered through Christ Life Ministries that I was blessed to be a part of during my own journey back) is to "equip people to be followers of Christ who live their lives with nothing to prove, nothing to lose, nothing to fear, and nothing to hide." How refreshing! In *The Ultimate Journey*, the authors illustrate the believer's own need to hide his or her messes through a game called "The Beach Ball."

Imagine an ocean filled with "godly-looking" Christians (whatever that is), bobbing up and down like Christ-filled corks. Underneath each secret sinner are large beach balls filled with a lot of "hot air."

"I am a perfect businessman because I am the CEO of my company."

"I am a perfect mom because I am the PTO president."

"I am a perfect teenager because I am the captain of our cheer leading squad."

Each ball represents the hidden sin in the life of each believer. The "hot air" is what we mask it with. The goal of the game is simple—to keep your beach ball, or secret sin, under the water. Not an easy task.

No matter how hard we try, the rolling waves birthed by the inevitable storms of life coupled with the sheer exhaustion of living a seemingly "perfect" life, eventually cause our shameful "sin ball" to pop to the surface. When that happens, we are met with judgmental stares from shocked onlookers who cannot believe we are anything less than "perfect."

Our shameful secret is offered up as a prayer request (or "godly" gossip) in small group time. Our Bible-believing circle of friends scatter to the wind, while our shameful sin spreads like wildfire amongst the congregation. Grace is rarely offered. Although everyone sins, your sin is perceived as worse. What was intended to be a Culture of Redemption has no redeeming qualities at all.

WELCOME TO THE "FISH-BOWL," MY FRIENDS. MULTIPLY THE WATER PRESSURE BY A MILLION, AND YOU ALMOST GET THE IDEA OF THE UNTOLD PRESSURES OF MARRIAGE IN MINISTRY.

Welcome to the "fishbowl," my friends. Multiply the water pressure by a million, and you almost get the idea of the untold pressures of marriage in ministry.

The Quest to Appear Perfect

During our first thirteen years of married ministry life, we moved from town to town and from church to church. At each church, we lived out our "private" life within the walls of a fragile glass house, or fishbowl, to an audience of judgmental congregations. The rolling reels of our own "reality show" played out larger than life to an audience of "godly" onlookers. I often imagined our Christian congregation slouched comfortably in cushy movie theater seating on our front lawn, munching away on freshly popped popcorn, sipping on their sodas, and anticipating our every move. In my stronghold mind, every move had to be "perfect."

Friendships were difficult to come by because few wanted to "hang out" with the pastor's family lest they be judged. Church "politics" left new scars with each departure, and I began to resent the ministry life of impossible perfection that I had married into. My husband was not "perfect." Our marriage was not "perfect." Our three sons were not "perfect." I could never be "perfect" enough.

In 2008, in what I believe was an effort to gain some sort of perfection in ministry, our "imperfect" family left the security of a successful local youth ministry to start a new church (a daunting task for any young family of five, let alone a wounded family). The pressure was on as members of our former congregation, which happened to be just one highway exit away, waited for our "crazy" family to fail. Because it was a church start, my husband assumed the role of pastor, and I assumed the role of everything else. With so much on my plate, it was impossible for ANY of it to be "perfect." Life was spinning out of control.

In reality, our "reality show" of perfection was not reality at all. The non-stop Bible studies, meetings, weddings, funerals, baptisms, counseling, events, and overall demands of the church were weighing heavy on our marriage. The children and I became second place to the church, and therefore, my relationship with the Lord

MY HUSBAND WAS HAVING AN AFFAIR WITH THE CHURCH, AND I HAD HAD ENOUGH.

became last place in my life. I resented Him, the church, and ministry in general.

My husband was having an affair with the church, and I had had enough.

In a desperate attempt to maintain control, I poured myself more and more into my professional career. I valued anything or anyone who valued me. The false sense of love, acceptance, and "celebrity status" I earned from my professional peers seemed to fill the empty spaces of my heart. Idols of performance and perfection from my childhood, sculpted my mind with a false sense of security.

I became a "human doing" instead of a "human being." The problem was, I could never DO enough. And because I could never DO enough, depression gradually took over.

I was a God-fashioned piece of pottery balancing on the edge of the altar. Because divorce was not an option in our "perfectly" painted portrait of a ministry marriage, I desperately began searching for an escape—a way out. I spent my days fantasizing of a pressure-free life outside the restrictive walls of a ministry marriage. Satan, who had studied my weak areas for a lifetime, knew my addiction to performance and perfection. I believed the lifelong lie that "I was not enough."

If I could not be perfect, I had no business being a pastor's wife. Maybe I had married the wrong person? After all, I did not fit the stereotypical mold of an organ-playing pastor's wife. I did not even like the organ.

Perhaps the grass really WAS greener on the other side. What was the harm in looking?

In July 2010, while traveling home from a training Seminar for my professional career, Brian encouraged me to join Facebook. For months, I had stubbornly drug my feet on the idea after witnessing the addictive nature and wasteful time spent on what I deemed an "electronic form of a brag book." He pitched that it would be a great way to build my business and reconnect with friends from the past.

Although his motives were pure, my heart was not. Unbeknownst to him, I joined that day to escape. When the practicality of social media collided with the escape route I had developed in my mind, fantasy became my reality. With just a couple of key strokes, I was gone.

Reflections at the Well

What is your Scarlet Letter "A" or "Beach Ball?"

How are we to overcome our shame, according to Revelation 12:11, and why is this so difficult?

How could the Lord use your "mess" as your "message?"

*End your time at the Well by praising the Lord, through prayer, for your "messes" and His shed blood that washes you white as snow. Then, declare to Him, "I **will** overcome by Your blood and the word of my testimony!"*

Section Two:

BROKEN

Chapter 4

JUDGMENT DAY

—◦◦◦✝◦◦◦—

The Lord himself goes before you and will be with you;
he will never leave you nor forsake you.
(Deuteronomy 31:8)

T he defendant reluctantly entered the courtroom, took her seat on the witness stand and stared smugly in the face of the prosecutor. After clearing his throat, the prosecutor began his line of questioning to an audience of just two jurors.

"Is there something you need to tell me?" he asked the defendant.

Much to his disappointment, there was nothing but silence from the witness stand.

"Is there?" he asked again, as if she had not heard him.

In silence, she shook her head, shrugged her shoulders and folded her arms in defiance.

"Lady and gentleman of the jury," he announced. "I present to you Exhibit A." And with that, the prosecutor held up a Facebook profile photo of "him," her accomplice—a man she knew all-too-well. Her heart sank.

"Do you know this man?" he asked the defendant.

The accused squirmed with discomfort in her seat, as the jurors leaned forward with anticipation of her reply.

After some hesitation, she answered with an almost irritated, "Yes."

"And how do you know him?" he pried, already knowing the answer to his question.

"He is a guy I went to high school with," she answered matter-of-factly. "I hardly know him."

"Oh really?" he sneered sarcastically. "Then, how do you explain this?"

The prosecutor proudly held up a yellow, flashing neon "sign" in the form of a highlighted piece of paper. The word "guilty" accompanied by an arrow below pointed straight at the defendant. The jurors gasped.

"Lady and gentleman of the jury," he explained, "I present to you Exhibit B, the defendant's phone bill. On this phone bill, you will find hundreds of text messages and phone calls during a two-month period between the defendant and the man she 'hardly' knows."

Judgmental stares from the jurors destroyed what little pride the defendant had left. No doubt, the evidence was damning.

"And, finally, do you know these little girls?" holding up his last piece of evidence, Exhibit C, a photo of her accomplice's three children, the accuser's eyes began to well up with tears.

She glanced at the photo and then quickly turned away, her heart

"TRACI, ARE YOU TRYING TO REPLACE OUR FAMILY?" BRIAN ASKED ME. I WILL NEVER FORGET THAT MOMENT OR THAT QUESTION. IT WAS AN APPROPRIATE QUESTION THAT I HAD NO ANSWER FOR.

breaking for the innocent victims involved on both sides.

"Yes," she whispered back as she stared down helplessly at her chained feet below. She wanted to run away, but could not. "Those are his daughters."

"Traci, are you trying to replace our family?" Brian asked me.

I'll never forget that moment or that question. It was an appropriate question that I had no answer for.

The jury took no time to deliberate. Why would they? My fate had already been sealed before I even entered the courtroom.

"We, the jury, find the defendant, Traci Smith, guilty of adultery in the first degree," they sneered while hurling their stones at the witness stand. "We sentence you to a life of shame, guilt, and total isolation."

Caught and Cast Out

All at once, I was a modern-day version of the biblical "woman caught in adultery," unwillingly brought forth and completely exposed for the sinner I was in the temple courts.

> *The teachers of the law and the Pharisees brought in a woman caught in adultery. They made her stand before the group and said to Jesus, "Teacher, this woman was caught in the act of adultery. In the Law Moses commanded us to stone such women. Now what do you say?"* (John 8:3-6)

In truth, I had been sentenced by my own pious Pharisees to death row, with no possibility of parole. The verdict came down on me like a life-sized gavel, obliterating what was left of my life to pieces.

"How could you do this to our family?" Brian wept.

Ironically, in my sin-stained state of mind, all I could think about was, "How could he do this to me? How dare he accuse me in this way—in front of these people and in this place? He is just as guilty of adultery as I am."

Just thirty minutes earlier, Brian had met me at the close of my weekly business meeting, which happened to be held in the back offices of the same exact shopping center that our church met in.

"When you are finished, come meet me at the church," he said. "I want to talk to you."

As he walked away, I suspected something was wrong. He had never interrupted my meeting before. As I made the seemingly long, yet physically short, walk down the sidewalk adjoining the church and my office, I was confused to see several cars parked outside. Mondays were not a typical night for church events. And although my gut was telling me to "turn back" or "make a run for it," I did not listen.

In the distance, I could hear the faint shouts of Satan and his team of thugs, "Move aside! Dead woman walking!"

Minutes later, I found myself "chained" to a makeshift witness stand (our church Welcome Center sofa) in a makeshift courtroom (our church lobby) in front of two makeshift jurors (a husband and wife who were members of our church). I was enraged. The same church that had stolen away my husband in its own sinful act of adultery was now preparing to stone me to death.

Just one week earlier, I had confessed my adulterous relationship to a "trusted friend," the wife and juror who now sat beside me on the sofa. I stared at her with utter disgust. I had been betrayed by the one person I had confided in. Incidentally, she also was caught in the thick of adultery herself. Apparently, the "if any one of you is without sin, let him be the first to throw a stone at her" rule did not apply to her.

THE SAME CHURCH THAT HAD STOLEN AWAY MY HUSBAND IN ITS OWN SINFUL ACT OF ADULTERY WAS NOW PREPARING TO STONE ME TO DEATH.

"I have packed a suitcase for you." All at once, Brian's voice cut through the noisy storm in my head, bringing me back to the harshness of my reality. "You are not welcome in our home anymore."

"Where am I supposed to go?" I pled in desperation. "I do not have any place to go."

"As long as you do not go to him, I do not care where you go," he answered hurling his first stone. "But you are not welcome in our home anymore. Your suitcase is in the sanctuary."

"In the sanctuary?" Apparently, our once sacred sanctuary where we worshipped at the feet of a grace-filled God had morphed into a luggage storage unit for the condemned.

Solitary Confinement

As I shuffled my way in shackled feet out of our church lobby, through the luggage depot and to my "new normal" of "solitary confinement," I was met by my first of several prison guards.

My sister, who lived two hours away, stood steadfastly between me and the church exit.

"What are you doing?" she screamed as she cast her stone. "You are ruining your life!"

"Get out of my way," I pushed against her. "I am leaving!"

"Where are you going?!"

"Get out of my way," I repeated. "I am leaving!"

"No, you are not," she said as she pushed me away from the exit with a righteous anger.

Like a caged animal, I lashed out with sharp claws. "Move out of my way!" I screamed shoving her to the ground with a defiant growl. I pushed open the church exit and escaped down the sidewalk toward my office, suitcase and car keys in hand. My coworkers watched in confusion as my sister chased after me.

I was surprised in the back of the building by local police who met me at my car with flashing lights. My sister had called the cops out of concern for my erratic behavior. After questioning Brian, the "jurors," my sister and me, the police confiscated my car keys and asked that I be escorted to a safe and secure location—my parent's weekend home, which would be my "prison" for the next twenty-four hours.

I was guarded by two appointed church members—my sofa "Judas" who drove me from the church to the prison, and another woman, both of whom questioned me relentlessly and seemed to empathize with my desperate circumstances. Secretly, they relished in the "godly" gossip offering complimentary counsel, which I politely declined given my lack of trust in their motives.

AFTER QUESTIONING BRIAN, THE "JURORS," MY SISTER AND ME, THE POLICE CONFISCATED MY CAR KEYS AND ASKED THAT I BE ESCORTED TO A SAFE AND SECURE LOCATION— MY PARENT'S WEEKEND HOME, WHICH WOULD BE MY "PRISON" FOR THE NEXT TWENTY-FOUR HOURS.

Sentenced to Therapy and a Psychiatric Ward

Brian ordered that I was to have no contact with the outside world, specifically "him," and therefore, my phone was confiscated. My parents, who had driven three hours through the night from their hometown of San Antonio, took the morning shift of guarding their deranged daughter. They would later drive me to an emergency counseling session that included Brian, my therapist, and myself.

"My wife is sick," Brian explained to my therapist. "She needs help."

"I am not sick" I argued. "I just do not love you anymore. I am not sure I ever did."

Accusatory arrows and insidious insults hurled across the smallness of my therapist's office. The firing squad was out in full force that Tuesday—hurtful words from hurting people. Although Brian insisted that he had "forgiven" me, his actions showed me otherwise. Instead of owning up to his guilt in the matter of Brian Smith vs. Traci Smith (his own adulterous affair with the church), he firmly believed that I was solely at fault. After all, I was "sick."

The only way to prove his accusations untrue, that I was not "sick" but rather desperately "sad," was to sentence myself to a ten-day intensive out-patient program at a Houston area psychiatric hospital for evaluation. So, I did. I entered a plea of "insanity."

Sin steals everything. In twenty-four hours, I lost everything—my husband, my children, my home, and my integrity. So called "friends" scattered to the winds due to rumors of my "mental illness" and hospitalization. My new friends, the ones that I surprisingly felt safest around because they did not try to "fix" me, were bipolar, schizophrenic, and homicidal. They understood the pain of rejection, and showed me more mercy than my own "Christian" church.

MY NEW FRIENDS, THE ONES THAT I SURPRISINGLY FELT SAFEST AROUND BECAUSE THEY DIDN'T TRY TO "FIX" ME, WERE BIPOLAR, SCHIZOPHRENIC, AND HOMICIDAL.

No one understands mercy more than those who need it the most.

After ten days, I was discharged from the hospital with my diagnosis being "major depressive disorder." My psychiatrist, who never fully understood why I was admitted, scratched his head and said, "You are not *mentally ill.* You are just unhappy in your marriage." At last, I was vindicated.

Sadly, it was too late. On my way home from the hospital, Brian called to inform me that he had filed for divorce.

The Ends

At that moment, I became a fugitive on the run. My marriage was over. I did not know what to do or where to go. So, out of sheer desperation, I ran to the one person in whom I believed I could trust—"him." Paranoia set in, and I ran to "safety."

The funny thing was that I did not feel "safe" at all. Although we spent the day driving around his small town dreaming of a future together, history had convinced me that I was being followed. In my spirit, I felt unsettled, empty, and exhausted. Our last moments together ended abruptly when the doorbell rang.

My dad, accompanied by a church elder, had come to confront my oppressor and escort me back to my hometown. In a strange way, I was relieved. My long saga of secrecy was finally over. I quickly grabbed my belongings and said my final face-to-face "goodbye" to the man who claimed to "love" me, but never really did. While I was in the hospital, he had married someone else.

I QUICKLY GRABBED MY BELONGINGS AND SAID MY FINAL FACE-TO-FACE "GOODBYE" TO THE MAN WHO CLAIMED TO "LOVE" ME BUT NEVER REALLY DID.

During our divorce mediation in May 2011, our mediator, who had never met us before, spoke a word over Brian as he sat alone with his attorney.

"Your marriage will not end in divorce," she said. "God will restore this marriage for His glory."

At the same time, in a room just around the corner, my attorney spoke a word over me, "You and your husband have the opportunity to choose each other again."

Although Brian and I attempted to reconcile during a brief summer "probation" period, which included a marriage renewal proposal at the top of New York's Empire State building and a family vacation to Florida's Disney World, I shamefully became a "repeat offender." Although this affair only lasted two weeks, our marriage did not recover.

Like half of all ministry marriages, we became another casualty of spiritual warfare, divorcing in September 2011.

Our marriage of sixteen years was over, or so we thought.

Reflections at the Well

Have you ever been caught in the middle of sin? If so, how were you treated?

What do you think sinful women need the most?

Read the story of the "woman caught in the act of adultery" (John 8:3-6). What did Jesus say to those who were prepared to stone her? What do you think Jesus would say today to those prepared to stone you for your sins?

End your time at the Well by praising the Lord, through prayer, for His redemptive love. He casts no stones at you.

Chapter 5

IT IS NOT TOO LATE

Be still before the Lord and wait patiently for him. (Psalm 37:7)

I n May 2014, my husband and I attended a ministry conference at Quest Community Church in Lexington, Kentucky, called The Uprising. To be honest, we attended partially out of curiosity, but mostly out of guilt. Our longtime ministry friends had been inviting us to participate for years, and we had finally run out of excuses. I had NO expectations whatsoever, and I was most excited about some well-deserved time away from work and the kids. My plan was simple—rest and relaxation.

But God had different plans.

Because you and I have just met, this next "bit" will be news to you. I am going to let you in on a little secret (I know what you are thinking—not another secret). I have always had a God-given dream to write a book (emphasis on the words "God-given"). I guess you could say it was "in my blood" from the beginning. You see, my mom's dad owned his own trade magazine. I can still remember, as a little girl, standing in awe of the large layout tables covered in paper scraps and smelling of rubber glue.

Growing up, writing always came naturally. Give me an essay test any day of the week, and I could write my way to an "A" like nobody's business. Writing was always my "out"—a way of escape from what pained me. Through writing, I could express myself. I could be anything and say anything with total freedom.

Writing became such a passion in my life that I actually chose it as a career. In 1995, I graduated from Texas A&M University with a degree in Journalism, and was offered my first writing job fresh out of college as the editor of an international religious newspaper in the Houston area.

Although God would allow me just a short season in this career, the desire to write a book never ever escaped me. But because I believed the lie that I did not have a story to tell, I carelessly discarded my dream in the pile marked "someday."

As God would have it (no "luck" here), a Christian publishing company "happened" to be at the "The Uprising" conference. After briefly "pitching" my story of sexual sin, brokenness, and restoration to them, they excitedly asked to publish "my book" (it is SO cool to finally say that), this very book that you are reading right now.

At the conference, the pastor of Quest, Pete Hise, debuted his first book titled *What Life Are You Waiting For?* In his book, Pastor Pete declares that "someday is a cuss word." In order for you to "push play" on the adventure God has for you, you must say an *instant yes*, followed by *immediate action* and absolutely *no negotiating*.

In that brief meeting with my soon-to-be editor, I said an instant *yes* and followed it with immediate action. Then I began negotiating. I can remember asking my husband, "There are so many women who have committed adultery. Why am I the 'lucky one' to write a book about it?"

His answer was simple, "Because you are willing."

I will never forget the Conference's closing session. Standing center stage was a single wooden cross with a simple sign nailed to it that read "It is not too late." One by one, Quest Community Church members crossed the stage to nail their God-given dreams or desires, once and for all, to the cross in total surrender. It is not too late...

- For hope
- Broken marriages
- The broken-hearted
- To say yes
- To make an impact
- For a resurrected heart
- To believe again
- For second chances
- For my friends
- For addicts
- For my football team
- To be forgiven

It is not too late "to be forgiven." Wow. Is that really true? Even for someone "like me?"

How many times have you asked yourself that very question? I can guess, as a fellow card-carrying member of the Christians Shamed by Sin Society, it is far too many times to count.

Pastor Pete ended the session with an "altar call" of sorts, recounting the story of the Israelites crossing the Red Sea. As they stood hopeless at the edge of the sea, just

IT IS NOT TOO LATE "TO BE FORGIVEN." WOW. IS THAT REALLY TRUE? EVEN FOR SOMEONE "LIKE ME?"

after being released from forty years in captivity, they griped out (notice I did not say "called out") to the God of the Universe about His ridiculous dead-end escape plan.

"Didn't we say to you in Egypt, 'Leave us alone; let us serve the Egyptians? It would have been better for us to serve the Egyptians than to die in the desert!'" (Exodus 14:12). Are you kidding me? You just escaped tyranny and now you want to go back? In some weird way, I get what the Israelites were thinking.

When caught or "enslaved" in the sticky web of sin, Satan tries to devour us through the lie of "it is too late." Somehow, we convince ourselves that the pain of regret is far easier than the pain of discipline. In other words, you have already screwed up way too much to start over in full and complete forgiveness.

WHEN CAUGHT OR "ENSLAVED" IN THE STICKY WEB OF SIN, SATAN TRIES TO DEVOUR US THROUGH THE LIE OF "IT IS TOO LATE."

Moses' answer to the Israelites' complaints is unexpected. "Do not be afraid. Stand firm and you will see the deliverance the Lord will bring you today. The Egyptians you see today you will never see again. The Lord will fight for you; you need only to be still" (Exodus 14:13-14).

Be still. Easy enough. Or is it? My experience has been that when everything seems to be falling apart, one of the hardest things to do is to "be still." In our flesh, we want to fix it. And the sooner, the better. Looking back on my restoration journey, I can remember that very moment when I was asked to "be still."

My Broken, Shamed, and Alone Moment—*What Is Yours?*

Once the movers had driven away, and I was left all alone in the emptiness of my new, lifeless post-divorce rented house, I was forced to "be still." This was my "moment." Broken, shamed, and alone.

What was yours? You know—that moment when you finally realized the destructive path you were on and the full weight of your sin. Maybe you have not had it yet? Or maybe it is now. In that moment, all you can do is "be still" because you have no idea what to do. In that moment, you would do anything to take it all back. But, you can't.

For me, all I could do, in my moment, was fall to my knees in humble surrender. I buried my head in the carpet, sobbed uncontrollably, and asked God for an "escape plan." In my flesh, I wanted it to be fast and easy. But in truth, the journey back would take years of humbling discipline from a Father who loved me more than I ever realized.

IN THAT MOMENT, ALL YOU CAN DO IS "BE STILL" BECAUSE YOU HAVE NO IDEA WHAT TO DO. IN THAT MOMENT, YOU WOULD DO ANYTHING TO TAKE IT ALL BACK. BUT, YOU CAN'T.

"The Lord disciplines those he loves, as a father the son he delights in" (Proverbs 3:12). Because He delights in me, in us, He takes the time to discipline us. As a mom, I can remember saying countless times, "this hurts me more than it hurts you," as I disciplined my sons' actions with a swift spank from "the spoon." In that moment, they could not see it as love. I do not know who cried more—me or them.

I am in no way trying to compare my pain to His, but perhaps this is exactly how our heavenly Father felt as He watched His one and only Son endure a most painful and shameful death on the cross. "This hurts me more than it hurts you," I can imagine Him saying as He watched the nails being hammered into His Son's hands.

Even at that moment, when all was empty and still, it was not too late. Even in death, Christ would have the ultimate victory, so that we, no matter how shamed and sinful, could ultimately have victory. "For Christ also suffered once for sins, the righteous for the unrighteous, to bring you to God. He was put to death in the body but made alive in the Spirit" (1 Peter 3:18).

AS WOMEN SHAMED BY SEXUAL SIN AND BROKENNESS, WE OFTEN FIND OURSELVES STANDING AT THE EDGE OF OUR OWN RED SEA, EMPATHIZING AND SYMPATHIZING WITH THE VERY SIN THAT ENSLAVES US, DEFENDING IT TO THE BITTER END.

Perhaps the Israelites who stood at the edge of the Red Sea were the original victims of the Stockholm syndrome. Wikipedia describes Stockholm syndrome as "a psychological phenomenon in which hostages express empathy and sympathy and have positive feelings toward their captors, sometimes to the point of defending and identifying with them."

As women shamed by sexual sin and brokenness, we often find ourselves standing at the edge of our own Red Sea, empathizing and sympathizing with the very sin that enslaves us, defending it to the bitter end. "Leave us alone," we say in the midst of our traumatic Stockholm syndrome bonding. "Let us serve our own brokenness through sexual sin. It would be better for us to serve our brokenness through sexual sin than to be healed!"

God says "Move on. Raise your staff and stretch out your hand over the sea to divide the water so that the Israelites (you) can go through the sea on dry ground...The Egyptians (all) will know that I am the Lord when I gain glory through Pharaoh, his chariots and his horsemen" (Exodus 14:15-16, 18).

In other words, even when you think it is too late, "it is not too late." You CAN be forgiven and you CAN move on. But to do so, action is always required. Just as I did that day at The Uprising, you must be willing to move out of your seat, walk the long aisle, ascend the steps, and stand in complete surrender to the adventure He has for you—an adventure that will ultimately give Him glory.

It is not too late to change. Change begins with true repentance.

Reflections at the Well

What does Exodus 14:13-14 tell us to do when we think "it is too late?"
What does it mean to "be still?"
Are you willing to "move on" (Exodus 14:15-16)? If so, what does that look like?

End your time at the Well by asking the Lord, through prayer, for your next steps. Then, be still and silent before Him, so that you can hear His instructions. If you are being "disciplined" at this moment because of your sins, thank the Lord that He loves you enough to discipline you.

Chapter 6

GOLF AND REPENTANCE

If we confess our sins, he is faithful and just and will forgive us our sins and purify us from all unrighteousness. (1 John 1:9)

I hate golf. There, I said it. Now before you burn this book in golf-devoted homage, let me explain.

My grandpa loved golf. In fact, he loved it so much that holidays were spent quietly watching him "watching" golf in his mustard-yellow leather recliner. Even he fell asleep at the sheer doldrums of this ridiculously slow-paced sport. The whispers of the commentators alone are enough to send any energetic person into a comatose, cross-eyed state.

Ironically, the day our divorce was finalized, my parents took me to see a movie about golf. Given my total lack of affection for the game, I was less than amused. I have to admit it was not at the top of my "I just-ended-a-sixteen-year-marriage-to-do" list.

I had no idea how profoundly impacted I would be by those ninety-eight minutes. The movie, *Seven Days in Utopia*, is based on a book authored by psychologist Dr. David Lamar Cook. After a disastrous debut on the pro circuit, a young golfer named Luke Chisholm finds himself unexpectedly stranded in Utopia, Texas, where he is welcomed by an eccentric rancher. The rancher, Johnny Crawford, challenges the broken and defeated Luke to "spend seven days in Utopia." By doing so, Johnny promises that he will help him "get his game back."

The movie is filled with poetic imagery and juicy tidbits, but one scene in particular had me in an utter "cry-like-a-baby" state. During Luke's seventh day in Utopia, Johnny sends his young protégé on one last self-discovery quest at the most unusual of places—the local Utopia Cemetery (like watching a golf movie after finalizing a divorce).

At the cemetery, Luke is instructed to write down all the lies that had been spoken over him throughout his lifetime. Lies that he had chosen to believe about himself. Lies based on sin. Once the list was made, Luke was to "bury" those lies at the foot of a tombstone engraved with three simple letters: SFT. See His face. Feel His presence. Trust His love. Before leaving, Luke was to "unearth" the truth, God's Truth, about who He really was. Bury the lies. Unearth the truth.

TRUE REPENTANCE COMES FROM NOT SIMPLY SAYING, "I AM SORRY," BUT FROM CHOOSING TO TURN AWAY FROM YOUR SINFUL PAST TO HEAD LASER-FOCUSED IN THE OPPOSITE DIRECTION.

This reminds me a lot of repentance. True repentance comes from not simply saying, "I am sorry," but from choosing to turn away from your sinful past to head laser-focused in the opposite direction.

Jesus said it best to the woman caught in adultery, "Go, and sin no more" (John 8:11).

Easier said than done, especially when it comes to the addictive nature of sexual sin. James, Jesus' own brother, explains the temptation of sin in this way, "But each person is tempted when they are dragged away by their own evil desire and enticed. Then, after desire has conceived, it gives birth to sin; and sin, when it is full-grown, gives birth to death" (James 1:14-15).

Even on that first night in my post-divorce home, when I found myself crying face down on the carpet seemingly alone (just me and God), I did not yet have a truly repentant heart. I wish I could say that I did. But, in many ways, I had not fully hit "rock bottom." The pull of my own evil desire for sexual sin was still there. In some ways, it was stronger than ever.

ALTHOUGH I APPEARED TO HAVE "MOVED ON" WITH THIS OTHER MAN, I WAS REALLY JUST "STICKING A BAND-AID" ON A WOUND THAT HAD NEVER REALLY HEALED—A WOUND STEMMING ALL THE WAY FROM MY CHILDHOOD.

In fact, just a month after our divorce, I fell into temptation again by beginning a physical and serious relationship with yet another man. He was a fellow divorcee, and I justified my actions with thoughts like, "I am not married anymore, so technically, this is not adultery." My desire gave birth to sin, which ultimately gave birth to death—death of my marriage.

Although I appeared to have "moved on" with this other man, I was really just "sticking a Band-Aid" on a wound that had never really healed—a wound stemming all the way from my childhood. I was treating my "symptoms" with another "false" relationship grounded in sex, instead of tackling my "illness" head on with complete and total repentance.

When it comes to pain in our lives (caused by our own actions or the actions of others), we all tend to avoid the hard work of "owning" the illness, and instead "numb out" through sinful "feel good" addictions like drugs, alcohol, food, work, and more. For me, my "medication of choice" was sex.

Moving into a new relationship before true repentance was a catastrophic mistake. Not only had I quickly moved on, but Brian began a relationship as well. In fact, when word got out about the new single pastor in town, our church attendance increased dramatically. "Christian" women showed up in "herds," placing bets on who would win the affection of the most eligible Christian man in town.

Soon after our divorce, the Lord led both Brian and I, separately, to a nationwide, non-denominational mercy ministry called *Divorce Care,* which was being offered at a local church. During this thirteen-week course, an entire week's lesson is devoted to "New Relationships." The study strongly discourages new relationships, encour-

CHANGE MUST HAPPEN BEFORE TRUE RESTORATION CAN TAKE PLACE. BUT, CHANGE ONLY COMES FROM TRUE REPENTANCE.

aging the wounded participant to be content with singleness through love and satisfaction in God alone. Moving on before discovering these truths can, not only deepen the divorcees' wounds, but it has the potential to deeply wound the people with whom they are involved.

Change must happen before true restoration can take place. But, change only comes from true repentance. David understood this. Although David was a betrayer, liar, adulterer and murderer, God refers to David in the Bible as "a man after my own heart" (Acts 13:22).

The Bible makes no effort to hide David's failures. In fact, thanks to biblical scribes, his sins are forever engraved in bold black letters against a pure white backdrop. Generations will read them and judge him by them. David had every reason to believe that the "lie" of once an adulterer always an adulterer spoken over him for years would always define him. Had he not repented, this would most likely be the case.

David, more than anything, had an unshakeable belief in a faithful and forgiving God. A God who chooses to see us pure and blameless just like David, through "blood-colored" glasses when we humbly repent. He says to our courtroom of jurors and judges, "My Son has cancelled the record containing the charges against her. Now, go and sin no more."

Although David sinned many times, he was quick to confess his sins. His confessions were from the heart, and his repentance was genuine. "Have mercy on me, O God, according to your unfailing love; according to your great compassion blot out my transgressions. Wash away all my iniquity and cleanse me from my sin" (Psalm 51:1-2). When pursuing true repentance, praying these same words can be a powerful starting point.

The consequences of David's choice to give in to desire and commit adultery with Bathsheba were far-reaching, affecting many others. His sin led to the murder of Bathsheba's husband and, ultimately to the death of David and Bathsheba's child. David never took God's forgiveness for granted. In return, God never held back from David His forgiveness or the consequences of his actions.

Unlike David, we would rather avoid the consequences of our sexual sin than experience forgiveness. Once sin gets started, it is hard to stop. The deeper the mess, the less we want to admit having caused it. We play the "blame game," blaming our circumstances or past for our own willingness to sin again and again.

WE PLAY THE "BLAME GAME," BLAMING OUR CIRCUMSTANCES OR PAST FOR OUR OWN WILLINGNESS TO SIN AGAIN AND AGAIN.

A year ago, our family of five grew to six overnight when we invited a 17-year old, homeless teen to come and live with us. Our motives, although suspicious to his less-than-loving family, were pure and simple—to give him a "hope and future" in the safety of a stable Christian home environment. Due to life circumstances, he had "bounced" from abusive parents to foster care to juvenile detention to alcoholic relatives and finally to the streets.

Being raised in nothing but dysfunction, he had a history of making poor choices, "numbing out" through such "vices" as drugs, alcohol, and sex. No doubt, he could easily blame his sins on his circumstances and past. Although he saw no "hope and future" for himself, we believed differently.

Teaching love through boundaries to a teen who has never had boundaries before has been the greatest challenge thus far. To this day, he continues to push back and chooses to follow his own set of "rules." The more he follows his own rules or desires, the more he gives birth to sin. Instead of true repentance, he attempts to justify his actions by blaming others. Sadly, he has not hit "rock bottom" yet. Repentance is not even on the radar.

Which begs the question, "How much mercy is too much mercy?" Honestly, we ask ourselves this question daily. If he continues down this destructive path, giving in to his sinful desires and then justifying them by blaming others, his future looks very grim. He often tells us, "I want to change. I promise I will change." But words are empty if not followed by true repentance. Until he "owns" his sin and decidedly turns away, change will never happen.

Pharaoh, too, had an unrepentant heart. When hit by plague after plague, Pharaoh finally admits his sin, "'This time I have sinned,' he said to them. 'The Lord is in the right, and I and my people are in the wrong. Pray to the Lord, for we have had enough thunder and hail. I will let you go. You don't have to stay any longer'" (Exodus 9:27-28).

After promising to let the Hebrews go, Pharaoh immediately broke his promise and brought even more plagues on the land. His actions, like our unrepentant son, reveal that his repentance was not real. "As long as we go on sinning," we do damage to ourselves and to others. Pretending to change is not change at all. "Dear friends, if we deliberately continue sinning after we have received knowledge of the truth, there is no longer any sacrifice that will cover these sins" (Hebrews 10:26 NLT).

David, on the other hand, chose not to sin repeatedly. He learned from his mistakes because he accepted the suffering that they brought. Although David had sinned with Bathsheba, David knew, most importantly, that he had sinned against God.

In today's multimedia world of "reality" television shows, movies and chat rooms, adultery is glorified. It is acceptable if no one gets hurt. But the truth is, everyone gets hurt. The ripple effects are astronomical. In David's case, a man was murdered and a baby died.

All sin hurts us and others, but ultimately it offends God because sin is rebellion against God.

ALL SIN HURTS US AND OTHERS, BUT ULTIMATELY IT OFFENDS GOD BECAUSE SIN IS REBELLION AGAINST GOD.

The good news is this—no sin is too great to be forgiven! Because David earnestly repented of his sins, God mercifully forgave him. God offers the same forgiveness to you. It starts with true repentance.

Experiencing True Forgiveness

My true repentance came just seven months following our divorce during Spring Break. It was my "holiday" to have the boys, and we chose to spend it at my uncle's ranch in the Texas hill country. On the way to the ranch, my family stopped in a little town called Utopia, Texas.

There was a rumor that a "Buried Lies Cemetery" had been created in honor of the movie that made this once unknown town famous. Of course, my family had to see if the rumor was true. Sure enough, just off the main street down a winding country road was a tree-covered cemetery lined with headstones. Between the actual cemetery and the Links of Utopia Golf Course (also made famous in the film), was a large rectangular sand pit labeled "Buried Lies Cemetery."

The makeshift grave included a large headstone made out of white Central Texas limestone engraved with the letters "SFT." Several golf clubs were halfway buried in the sand. Next to the "cemetery" was an excerpt from the book along with a sign that read, "Bury your lies here." So, I did.

I could hardly see to write through the tears. But, I wrote them all down—all of the lies: "You are a whore. You are dirty. You are unlovable. No one will ever love you again." One by one, the lies were exposed for what they were. I crumbled them up, dug deep in the sand and buried them. And then, I prayed.

I do not remember exactly what I said, but I think it went something like this, "Have mercy on me, O God, according to Your unfailing love; according to Your great compassion blot out my transgressions. Wash away all my iniquity and cleanse me from my sin."

I closed my prayer with one simple plea, "Lord, I want my husband back. If You can, please restore my marriage."

"If I can?" said Jesus. "Everything is possible for one who believes" (Mark 9:23).

Reflections at the Well

What is "true repentance?" What would "go, and sin no more" look like in your life (John 8:11)?

In what ways have you "stuck a Band-Aid" on a wound that had never really healed? What is your medication of choice?

What lies spoken over you in your lifetime need to be "buried?"

End your time at the Well by "owning your sins" through prayer. Take ownership by confessing your sins against the Lord, accepting the suffering that they bring and repenting (or turning the opposite direction) to sin no more.

Chapter 7

HE POPPED THE QUESTION

When Jesus saw him lying there and learned that he had been in this con-dition for a long time, he asked him, 'Do you want to get well?'" (John 5:6)

Almost a year ago, I injured myself training for my third, yes third, marathon. It was an early, and I mean early, smoldering September Texas morning when I met my marathon team for a "quick," routine six-teen-mile run. The run had to be "quick," because the long-anticipated Texas A&M University verses Alabama football game was just hours away.

I can remember feeling really good that morning, and quite frankly, cranking out one of my best runs in my fourteen-year marathon racing career. After a quick shower followed by the weekly donning of my Aggie maroon best, I made my way to a tailgate party just blocks from Kyle Field.

Although I was a little sore, which was completely understandable given my stellar performance earlier that morning, I was no "two-per-center" (a term used for half-hearted Aggie fans). I happily made my way up the steep ramps to the third deck of the football stadium where I would watch my beloved Aggies get "outscored" by the opposing team (we do not "lose," we get "outscored.")

The very next morning, I "tried my feet" at a short, emphasis on "short," stretch run to work out the kinks. Much to my surprise, I could only manage to run one house over due to the excruciating pain that shot up the outside of my left foot and ankle. Something was definitely wrong.

After six months of medical analysis, it was determined that I had been running for years on a stress fracture. This untreated stress fracture had caused the cartilage between two bones to literally disintegrate. Those same two bones were now grinding against each other, which ultimately caused a cyst to form. The only solution to stop the pain was to surgically remove the cyst and "fuse" my bones on the top of my foot together with a plate and five screws.

It was a risky solution that could eliminate the pain, but remove all mobility in that one joint. Because of this, the pressure from any running in the future could transfer pain to other areas of my foot. This would lead to more surgeries and the possibility of never being able to run again.

The decision was up to me. Did I want to risk everything to get well? Or would I choose to just lay down on my mat and wallow in self-pity?

THE DECISION WAS UP TO ME. DID I WANT TO RISK EVERYTHING TO GET WELL? OR WOULD I CHOOSE TO JUST LAY DOWN ON MY MAT AND WALLOW IN SELF-PITY?

Flashback two thousand years to the temple in Jerusalem and a pool called Bethesda. "Here a great number of disabled people used to lie—the blind, the lame, the paralyzed. One who was there had been an invalid for thirty-five years. When Jesus saw him lying there and learned that he had been in this condition for a long time, he asked him, 'Do you want to get well?'" (John 5:3-6).

During my continuous restoration process (notice I said "continuous") from sexual sin and brokenness to purity and wholeness, I have encountered numerous sexually shamed women who have asked me for advice. I am all too happy to share my "steps" back, only to find that a week later they are calling or texting me at all hours of the night because they find themselves, once again, broken, depressed, and unable to move forward. They are stuck on their mat, unwilling to do what it takes to "get well."

I am now in my third month of physical therapy (six months out of surgery), and I am often reminded by my physical therapist that "Physical therapy is not a microwave. It is a crock pot."

The same goes for the restoration of women who struggle with sexual sin and brokenness. It is not a microwave. It is a crock pot. It all starts with the answer to a simple question, "Do you want to get well?"

Say a Sincere *Yes*

FOR ME, MY SINCERE YES CAME IN THE FORM OF A SINCERE PRAYER.

Jesus is "popping" this same question to you. "Do you want to get well," friend? The answer to this new-life-or-eternal-death question is the first step on your road to restoration. When your answer is a **sincere *yes***, you have begun your restoration. I know this because this is how my restoration journey began.

Believers know it as the conviction of the Holy Spirit. When we say a sincere yes to the invitation to make Jesus Christ the Lord of our life, the Holy Spirit comes as an "added" bonus to dwell within us. He "adds" to our lives the conviction to say "no" to the wrong things and "yes" to the right things.

So let's start at the very beginning, because it is a very good place to start (insert Sound of Music soundtrack here without the garb made out of curtains). For me, my sincere yes came in the form of a sincere prayer. To say a sincere yes to a changed life, whether it is the first time or the millionth time, take a moment to pray this prayer:

Lord Jesus, I confess that I am a sinner in need of a Savior. I sincerely repent and turn away from my adulterous past and sexual sin. I ask for your forgiveness. I DO want to get well. I believe you died for my sins and rose from the dead. Guide my life. Help me to say "yes" to the right things and "no" to the wrong things. I trust and follow you as my Lord and Savior. In Your Name I pray, Amen.

STOP BLAMING OTHERS

God's Word promises that "if we confess our sins, he is faithful and just and will forgive us our sins and purify us from all unrighteousness" (1 John 1:19).

Once you have said a sincere yes to "getting well," you must **stop blaming others.** This is not their sin; it is yours.

When Jesus asked the man at Bethesda the "get well" question, he

THIS IS NOT THEIR SIN; IT IS YOURS.

chose to blame others for his sin. "'Sir,' the invalid replied, 'I have no one to help me into the pool when the water is stirred. While I am trying to get in, someone else goes down ahead of me'" (John 5:7).

Good grief. Someone go get this dude a little "whine for his cheese." Really? In thirty-eight years, you could not crawl yourself to the edge of the pool to be ready for the next "stirring"? Give me, and the rest of the temple folks, a major break.

Just as Jesus had little sympathy for this man and his laundry list of excuses, my restoration began when I stopped blaming others for the sin in my life. The truth was, I had made the choice to sin, regardless of what happened with an adult growing up, with the boys in high school and college, my husband and my church, or "the other man."

The truth was this—my desire gave birth to sin and my sin gave birth to death.

Have you ever stopped to think about who or what YOU blame for your sexual sin? Is it sexual abuse, a bad marriage, or "the other man?" Take a moment to make a list below of those you blame for your sexual sin. This list will be integral in your healing as we use it, in a later chapter, to trace back to our pasts in order to understand ourselves and those who have wounded us.

We must stop blaming others because if we were to take an honest look at our past and the past of those who have wounded us, the "blame game" could go on forever. I am sure there are many unrepentant souls in hell who are still blaming others for their eternal demise.

Bottom line, it is time to "own" your sin.

Take Immediate Action Steps

Jesus says to the invalid man, to me and to you, "'Get up! Pick up your mat and walk,' (or dare I say run). At once, the man was cured; he picked up his mat and walked." Your sincere *yes* is demonstrated by taking **immediate action steps.**

For me, my seven God-given action steps, which incidentally spell out the word RESTORE, included:

Reaching up to the Lord

Embracing His forgiveness

Seeking help from peers and professionals

Tracking back to my past

Overcoming Satan's lies with the Truth

Reconciling with myself and others

Empowering others through service

I will discuss, in detail, all seven steps in this section of the book.

In the meantime take these immediate action steps:

Disconnect from All Social Media: For example, I knew Facebook was a stumbling block for me, so I disconnected by deactivating my account. What are the social media venues that you use to feed your sexual sin? Disconnect!

Block Phone Numbers and Email Accounts: One of the first steps I made to "get well" was to block "the other man's" phone number and email address, so there was no possible way for him to connect with me. In fact, because I knew and understood my weak areas, I blocked **all** men. Who do you need to block?

Stay Away from "Those" Places: You know the places I am talking about. The places where you and your lover met—the restaurants, parking lots, back roads, hotels, movie theaters, etc. Avoid them at all costs, even if it means being inconvenienced by driving out of your way. God's calling is rarely convenient, but it is so worth it.

GOD'S CALLING IS RARELY CONVENIENT. BUT IT IS SO WORTH IT.

Tell a Trusted Christian Girlfriend/Mother/Sister Your Decision to "Get Well": Ask her to pray for you. Instead of calling or texting "him,"

contact her instead. She will be the one to "hold your feet to the fire" by keeping you accountable to your "wellness" program. Understand that you do not need a "gossip" girlfriend to commiserate with you. Instead, you need someone to "speak the truth in love" to you. That is what a Christian accountability partner will do. Ask God for wisdom. Be careful who you choose. This one is important.

Stop Sinning

I love that the story of Jesus' healing the man at Bethesda does not end there. Later, Jesus found him at the temple. "See, you are well again," he told the man. "Stop sinning or something worse may happen to you." Before you begin your restoration steps, which I will discuss in detail in the next seven chapters, you must make a once-and-for-all decision to **stop sinning.** No more slippery slope or halfway sin-ning. Stop sinning, period.

I know what you are thinking, "Stop sinning? That is impossible." Let me ask you a question, if you were sitting on death row for murder and you were miraculously par-doned and released, would you even consider murder again once you were finally free? Of course not. Your continuous sexual sin is a "death sentence." You can stop, with the Lord's help, if you really want to get well.

NO MORE SLIPPERY SLOPE OR HALFWAY SINNING. STOP SINNING, PERIOD.

Begin with the above immediate action steps. Next, take a moment to consider the consequences of continuing to live in sin. If you do not stop, what will happen? Consider the cost by making a list or "trying on" the con-sequences of a life grounded in sexual sin—loss of your integrity, friends, family, marriage, kids, home, job, financial freedom, or worse yet, your health via a sexually transmitted disease. After "trying on" this tumultuous life, "try on" a life without sexual sin. What major differences do you see? Write them down, then choose. My gut tells me you will choose to stop sinning.

Keep in mind, unless you are the Lord himself (that role is already taken), you cannot be "perfect" in your own flesh. You will most likely make mistakes along your restoration road. The point is, you make a daily choice not to sin. Choose, instead, to change. The truth is, you can and will change.

10 Truths to Change

My editor and writing coach, Dr. Larry Keefauver, lists "10 Truths to Change" that, looking back, were integral to my own transformation and ultimate restoration:

1. *Change* means that to do something new, you must let go of something old. Do not let your past determine your future. Trust that God is doing a "new thing" in your life (Isaiah 43:19).

2. *Change* will cost you time, money, and relationships. Change does not happen overnight, but it does happen. You must be willing to do the work, no matter the cost. Trust me, the rewards are so worth it. Think crock pot not microwave (Luke 14:12).

3. *Change* requires new perspective, plans, process, and people. Ask for His perspective, follow His plan, know that it is a process, and stay around people who will sharpen you. His ways are always higher (Isaiah 55:8-9).

4. *Change* demands focus. Become laser-focused on the Lord. He is the Author and Finisher of our faith. What He starts, He always finishes. He will never leave you or forsake you (Hebrews 12:2).

5. *Change* precipitates a fight. Recognize your restoration for the spiritual battle that it is. You are fighting for your life with the

most skilled army behind you. Satan and his thugs have nothing on you. You already have the victory (Ephesians 6:10-13).

6. *Change* requires follow through and finishing the job. Go where you have never gone. Do what you have never done. Risk more than you ever have. Determine now to finish your restoration race (2 Timothy 4:7-8).

7. *Change* involves others. You need a solid team of godly mentors and fellow believers to throw on the "team jersey" and run this race with you (Psalm 1:1).

8. *Change* demands faith, hope, and love (1 Corinthians 13:13-17:1).

9. *Change* pushes us into God's presence and ceaseless prayer. Prayer changes everything. Enlist plenty of prayer warriors in your restoration army (2 Corinthians 3:17-18).

10. *Change* starts now (Isaiah 43:19).

Pick up your mat and walk! It is time.

Reflections at the Well

Do you want to "get well?" What is holding you back?
Who are you blaming for your willfully committed sins?
What immediate actions should you take to stop sinning?

*Now that you have prayed a "sincere yes," end your time at the Well by asking the Lord to show you what immediate actions **you** should take to stop sinning.*

Section Three

RESIN

Chapter 8

REACH OUT AND TOUCH

As Jesus was on his way, the crowds almost crushed him. And a woman was there who had been subject to bleeding for twelve years, but no one could heal her. She came up behind him and touched the edge of his cloak, and immediately her bleeding stopped. (Luke 8:42-44)

My middle son, Brayson, was born with a unique condition called Intrauterine Growth Retardation (IUGR). Although he was a full-term baby, he only weighed 4 pounds 6 ounces. He is a living, breathing miracle.

At thirty-eight weeks, I visited my doctor for a routine pregnancy check-up. I can remember not feeling my best that day, but then again what woman feels her best when she looks like a football linebacker and outweighs her husband. To be honest, I had a bad attitude. I was tired of making the hopeful forty-five minute drive to his office (with packed suitcase in trunk), only to be disappointed with those five little words, "It is not time yet."

The week prior, I had visited the hospital emergency room because I was concerned that I was leaking amniotic fluid— "a mother's instinct." Because the "litmus" test was inconclusive, I was frustratingly sent home with instructions to not return unless I was "gushing" (a lovely word image).

"When was the last time you felt your baby move?' my doctor asked while measuring my exposed belly at thirty-eight weeks.

"What do you mean?" I asked in shock as I lay confused on the cold examination table. "Is something wrong?"

"Your belly has not grown in several weeks," he answered matter-of-factly.

Then he turned to his nurse and whispered an order for an emergency ultrasound with an obstetrician specialist—the same specialist who had successfully delivered the once infamous Houston octuplets.

After asking me if I had been leaking amniotic fluid (do not get me started), the specialist delivered the most alarming news.

MY ONCE HEALTHY, FULLY-DEVELOPED CHILD WAS, ALL-AT-ONCE, "SICK" AND ON THE BRINK OF BEING "STILLBORN."

"Your placenta has failed. You have no amniotic fluid in your belly. You will be lucky if this baby is four pounds. Your baby is dying."

One by one, the bad news was delivered in pounding repetition, knocking the wind right out of me. I literally felt like I was having an "out-of-body" experience.

My once healthy, fully-developed child was, all-at-once, "sick" and on the brink of being "stillborn."

I was rushed to Houston's Methodist Hospital, where I waited five hours for an "emergency" C-section. Once in the operating room, the hospital was unable to find an anesthesiologist to assist with the surgery. So, I was wheeled back out of the OR, told to put my tennis shoes on, and walked hurriedly down Houston Medical Center's Fannin Street (in hospital gown only while a church member carried my IV bag behind me) to see if the neighboring hospital, St. Luke's, could deliver my baby.

Once the IVs were switched out, I was prepped again for surgery. Although, this time, an anesthesiologist was available, my epidural did not work. I painfully felt every cut across my belly. In an effort to save my baby, I was eventually "put to sleep" under heavy sedation.

Just before I fell asleep, I begged the Lord in total desperation, "Lord, please let me hear him cry. I just want to know he is alive." To my surprise, He honored my prayerful plea with the most incredible gift. Although I was completely sedated, I did hear Brayson's first cries. They were the most beautiful sounds I ever heard.

Brayson was rushed immediately to Texas Children's Hospital, where he remained in the Neonatal Intensive Care Unit (NICU) off and on for two months. I would wake up early every morning, make the forty-five minute drive to the hospital, where I would sit by his bedside, holding his tiny little hand through the plastic dome that encased his bed. I would imagine no wires, IVs, or machines—just the two of us sharing precious moments together. To help in his healing, I would often "kangaroo" with my little dude. I would tuck his fragile body inside my hospital gown and lay him gently across my bare chest. Skin to skin.

THERE WAS HEALING, FOR BOTH OF US, IN "THE TOUCH."

I would reach for him, and in his own unique way, he would reach for me. There was healing, for both of us, in "the touch."

Just like the "unclean" woman described in the book of Luke, touch was everything.

As Jesus was on his way, the crowds almost crushed him. And a woman was there who had been subject to bleeding for twelve years, but no

one could heal her. She came up behind him and touched the edge of his cloak, and immediately her bleeding stopped. (Luke 8:42-44)

In his early developmental years, Brayson was diagnosed with several neurological disorders, the most challenging being Sensory Integration Dysfunction (SID). According to Wikipedia, SID is "characterized by significant problems to organize sensation coming from the body and the environment which is manifested by difficulties in the performance in one or more of the main areas of life: productivity, leisure and play, or activities of daily living."

In Brayson's case, his SID requires excessive touching. We often use the word picture of a computer and mouse. When a computer is in "sleep mode," the mouse (Brayson) needs to be touched, or moved, to "wake up" the computer (his brain). Growing up, Brayson's skin was stroked with bristled brushes and he sat on a large beach ball at his school desk—all to stimulate or "heal" his brain. Touch was everything, just like the bleeding woman.

It Is in the Reach

Notice that in this passage, the woman reached for Jesus' cloak. But what Jesus did and said next was key in this teaching moment. "Who touched me?" Jesus asked (Luke 8:45). Certainly Jesus knew who had touched Him—He knew that someone had purposefully touched Him to receive some sort of healing. In truth, Jesus wanted the woman to step forward and identify herself. To let her slip away would have meant a lost opportunity for Jesus to teach her that His cloak was not magical.

It had been her faith-filled reach that healed her.

Jesus wants you and me, as women who struggle with sexual sin, to step forward unashamedly and identify ourselves for the sinners we are and for the healing we need. He wants us to reach for Him in faith. In doing so, we are healed.

In other words, in our restoration journey, it is not one more self-help book, Oprah episode, support group, Bible study, or church service that heals us. It is in the reach. The cloak was not magical. Your first step to RESTORE requires a relentless reach.

IT HAD BEEN HER
FAITH-FILLED REACH
THAT HEALED HER.

But what does that look like?

Soon after my divorce, my mom gave me one of those countertop Scripture calendars. You know the kind—the one adorned with disgustingly cute kittens or pretty, perfect flowers. Each day you flip the page in an effort to mark the calendar date and to read your daily dose of Scripture. It is all a great idea. The truth was, my calendar sat dusty in the corner of my bathroom counter.

For the longest time, I could not bring myself to even turn the page, let alone look in the bathroom mirror. I was too ashamed. In my deep state of post-divorce and dirtied depression, it was all I could do to even get out of bed in the morning. On most days, I buried my entire body under the covers, flanked on either side by my Dachshund & Chihuahua (who in my mind, were the only ones who really understood me), and waited for the day to pass by. The bedroom blinds were always drawn shut to keep out as much light as possible.

Oh, I am speaking to someone now! You know who you are. You are lying in bed with the blinds drawn shut and probably have not bathed in days. If that is you, I want to encourage you to take baby steps. First, baby step your stinky self out of bed and open the blinds. Then, if you must, crawl back in to bed. Try that for the first few days. Then, for the next few days, open your blinds and crawl, if you must, to your bathroom, wash your face and brush your teeth. Do **not** go back to bed. After a few days of this activity, open your blinds, walk your way to the bathroom and take a shower. Again, do **not** go back to bed. Baby steps.

I am speaking from personal experience here because these were my baby steps. These baby steps eventually led to the most important baby step of all. One morning, I flipped the page on that countertop calendar. You could say, I reached. It was as if I was saying, "Okay God. I am bathed and dressed. Now what?"

I cannot tell you what day it was or even what Scripture I read. What I can tell you is that this "flip," this reach, was a significant step in my healing process. My faith-filled reach began with just reading the daily Scripture. Each was encouraging. Each was timely and on point. Each was like a soothing balm for my soul. It was as

IT WAS AS IF I WAS SAYING, "OKAY GOD. I AM BATHED AND DRESSED. NOW WHAT?"

if the Lord was romancing me in the most intimate way. Flip by flip, He was honoring my faith step with a little more healing.

Over time, reading just was not enough. So, I began meditating on those Words through a simple strategy called SOAP—Scripture, Observation, Application, and Prayer. The calendar moved from my bathroom to my bedside. Slowly and faithfully, I would wake up, open my bedroom blinds and let the Light of God's Word shine into my soul.

I began by reading the daily Scripture. I would write this Scripture at the top of my Quiet Time Journal page. Next, I would write out, in my own words, what this Scripture meant to me. Then, I would write out how

I could apply this Scripture to my life. Finally, I would incorporate this Scripture in prayer. SOAP. It was just enough food for my hungry soul. It was the "spiritual milk" in my daily cup of coffee. It was the "shot in the arm" I needed to make it through another day.

Let's give it a try. Below is an example of my daily Quiet Time:

(S)cripture- "'Daughter,' he said to her, 'be of good cheer; your faith has made you well. Go in peace'" (Luke 8:48).

(O)bservation- It was not the actual touch of Jesus' cloak that made the "unclean" woman well. It was her initial reach and faith that healed her. Healing brings peace.

(A)pplication- In order for me to heal from my sexual sin, I must reach for Jesus daily by meditating on His Word through faith. He must come first in my life. Jesus promises that my faith will make me well.

(P)rayer- *Father God, I praise you for your faithfulness! I confess that I have been unfaithful to you. I have not put you first in my life. I have turned to worldly solutions, instead of to your solution. I repent and ask your forgiveness. I thank you for your promise that "my faith will make me well," and wellness will bring me peace. I ask that you honor my faith steps, just as you honored this "unclean" woman. I want to get well. Help me. In Jesus' name, Amen.*

Notice that my prayer begins with Adoration (Praise), followed by Confession (Repentance), Thankfulness (Gratitude) and, finally, Supplication (Asking). This method of prayer, often referred to as ACTS, reminds me that prayer is more about my ACTion towards Him, then my asking of Him.

> *Then the woman, seeing that she could not go unnoticed, came trembling and fell at his feet. In the presence of all the people, she told why she had touched him and how she had been instantly healed.* (Luke 8:47)

Do you realize that with every reach you make, God's Word says that you are "instantly healed"? Every reach is met with an instant healing. So, reach!

Reflections at the Well

What does "touch" mean in your life?

Do you find yourself lying in bed with the blinds drawn shut? If so, what "baby steps" could you take to begin your restoration journey?

What does it mean to give yourself a daily "bath" through a daily Quiet Time?

End your time at the Well by applying the SOAP/ACTS method of Quiet Time with the Scripture noted in this chapter. Use this outline as a guide:

Scripture: "As Jesus was on his way, the crowds almost crushed him. And a woman was there who had been subject to bleeding for twelve years, but no one could heal her. She came up behind him and touched the edge of his cloak, and immediately her bleeding stopped" (Luke 8:42-44).

Observation: *In your own words, what is this Scripture saying?*

Application: *How can you apply this information in your own life?*

PRAYER:

Adoration: *What does this Scripture say about God? Use those words to praise Him.*

Confession: *How have you sinned against God today? Confess your sins to Him and ask for His forgiveness, which He gives freely.*

Thankfulness: *Write down three sentences describing three things you are thankful for today.*

Supplication: *Ask the Lord for what you need.*

Chapter 9

FLUENT IN FORGIVENESS

"Therefore, I tell you, her many sins have been forgiven—as her great love has shown. But whoever has been forgiven little loves little." (Luke 7:47)

Have you ever read the book *The Five Love Languages*? If not, allow me to summarize. In a nutshell, the book identifies five languages in which people express and receive love. The author, Dr. Gary Chapman, identifies these languages as: quality time, words of affirmation, gifts, acts of service, and physical touch.

Not-so-lucky for my husband, my love languages are gifts and words of affirmation. A week of missed flower gifting could most likely land him in a karaoke nightmare of a really bad rendition of "you don't bring me flowers anymore." When it comes to compliments, you better keep them coming, Mister. After all, a compliment a day keeps the nagging away.

In contrast, my husband's love languages are "quality time" and "touch." The two go hand in hand (no pun intended). Let's be honest, these two are most men's love languages of choice.

In a relationship, it is important to know and understand each other's love languages because if you express love toward the other in a way they do not understand, they will not realize you have expressed love at all. It would be like speaking a foreign language.

Speaking of foreign languages, it should be no mystery to you by now that I am a native Texan (I know what you are thinking, here we go again). One could say that I am a proud and somewhat obnoxious Texan (but what Texan is not proud and obnoxious?). Who could blame me? My family roots are so "deep in the heart of Texas" (yee haw) that I am actually directly related to the Commander of the Alamo, Colonel William Barrett Travis (my maiden name is Travis).

In fact, most of my family still lives in San Antonio. I love San Antonio for its cultural diversity and spicy Mexican heritage. Naturally, when it came time to decide which foreign language I would study in high school, I went with the obvious choice—French. What?! French?! *Oui Oui, mes amis.* (Translation: yes, yes, my friends.) Why on earth would I choose French when I lived in San Antonio with its huge Hispanic population?

I will tell you why—because French was romantic. As they say in Texas, that is "the gosh darn" truth. That is exactly why I chose it. It was romantic, and I am a hopeless romantic at heart.

My high school French teacher would tell you that my French "left something to be desired" (I am not even sure how to say that in French). I did not take the language seriously—a huge mistake when you choose to be an exchange student to France, which I did the summer after my high school senior year.

Other than a few catch phrases, I never really tried to learn French. This truth was exposed through the disgusted and confused looks from my French host family with every word that came out of my mouth. They were furious with me for not learning their language, and I was frustrated with them for demanding that I speak it. I am not 100 percent sure, but I think they referred to me as that "stupeed" American.

If there is one thing I learned from that experience it is—never let a native order your meal for you at a restaurant in France (note to self, "steak tar tar" is a raw hamburger patty). In order to truly connect with people, you must speak their language. (Okay, so maybe that is two things I learned.)

Don't you love it when people "get you?" You know what I mean, when they really accept, understand, and most importantly, love you for who you are. It is comforting when someone "speaks your language." Unfortunately, this is a rarity in today's sin-filled and self-hyphenated world. Love and acceptance are often based on claims and conditions.

With each "missed-pronounced" word of our love language, our spiritual savings account, or "love tank" is depleted. Constant withdrawals and debits from the "unforgiving" and "judgmental" leave us empty and bankrupt. It is an economic disaster.

But not in Jesus' economy. Jesus sees your zero balance and continues to credit it with deposit after deposit of unconditional love and acceptance.

Jesus always gets you.

Take a moment to get your mind around that—Jesus always gets you. He accepts you no matter what you have ever said or done. He understands

JESUS ALWAYS GETS YOU.

you more than anyone ever could. He loves you with an extravagant, everlasting, and unconditional love. He is crazy about you. He pursues you with a relentless love—a love framed in forgiveness.

Jesus' Love Language Is *Forgiveness*

About a month after my affair was exposed, Brian visited me at my parent's home. I will never forget that moment—the moment when he walked in to my parent's master bedroom where I lay practically lifeless in bed. In one hand, he held a bouquet of flowers, and in the other, his cell phone. He timidly climbed into bed alongside me, handed me the flowers, and nervously pushed play on his cell phone. The words of a familiar worship song cut through the awkward silence:

He will allure her. He will pursue her and call her out to the wilderness with flowers in His hand. She is responding, beat up and hurting, deserving death. But offerings of life are found instead.

All at once, this worship song by Shane & Shane, based on the book of Hosea and titled *Acres of Hope*, became a love song from a hurting husband to his broken bride. Just like the story of the prophet Hosea and his adulterous wife Gomer, Brian chose forgiveness and obedience over fury and offense.

The Lord said to me, "Go, show your love to your wife again, though she is loved by another man and is an adulteress. Love her as the Lord loves the Israelites." (Hosea 3:1)

Brian, with what little he had left, was singing a love song of forgiveness to me in the dialect of my two love languages—gifts and words of affirmation. Just as the lyrics and Scripture said, he was pursuing me with flowers in his hand. Sadly, I was not responding. At that moment, it was as if he was speaking a foreign language.

WHERE JESUS IS FLUENT IN FORGIVENESS; WE ARE FLUENT IN SHAME.

Women shamed and broken by sexual sin cannot hear clearly. It is as if our ears become clogged with the hardened mud of our own sinful dirtiness. We literally become deaf to the language of forgiveness, which is Jesus' love language to us. Where Jesus is fluent in forgiveness; we are fluent in shame.

Our Love Language to Jesus Is *Faith*

Just now I am reminded of the comedic film *Airplane*, and a scene in which a flight attendant is doing her best to communicate with two disgruntled passengers on the doomed flight. Unfortunately, she did not speak their language of "jive." Just then, a fellow passenger appears to the flight attendant and says, "Excuse me, Ms. I speak jive" (insert laughter here).

May I offer up my own biblical version of this scene (I know it is a stretch)? A forgiving Savior is doing His best to communicate with two shamed passengers aboard a one-way-trip to Shameville. All at once, a fellow sinner approaches the seats and says, "Excuse me, Jesus, I speak shame."

Ugh. How do we move past our shameful dialect to fluency in forgiveness? It all begins when we can come to a place of embracing the Lord's forgiveness. For me, this was **the** hardest thing to do. Before I could receive my husband's forgiveness, my children's forgiveness, and my own forgiveness toward myself, I had to receive the Lord's forgiveness.

But how?

Steps to Forgiveness Fluency

In Charles F. Stanley's, "The Gift of Forgiveness," he explains three steps to receiving God's forgiveness. These steps were significant in my "Rosetta Stone" translation study of forgiveness.

First, evaluate your view of God. For broken and shamed women, this view can be an extremely warped one—almost like looking in to a "fun house" mirror. Depending on our own distorted view of ourselves based on an earthly father's conditional love, we often view our heavenly Father's love for us in the same way—totally conditional. Take me as an example. From the beginning I learned that love was based on perfection and performance. These false lies of love, coupled with traces of childhood sexual abuse, warped my view of an all-loving God. God, to me, was a judgmental Father who expected me to look perfect and to perform perfect. He could **not** be trusted.

How about you? Has your earthly father's love tainted your view of God's love for you? I venture to guess that it has.

Secondly, examine what the Bible teaches about God's love. Broken and shamed women have a difficult time believing that God truly loves and forgives them. They are not the only ones. Even the Pharisees, who obeyed the strictest of religious laws in New Testament times, could not understand why Jesus associated with those they considered "sinners." "Now the tax collectors and 'sinners' were all gathering around to hear him. But the Pharisees and the teachers of the law muttered, 'This man welcomes sinners and eats with them'" (Luke 15:1-2).

Jesus responded to the "muttering" Pharisees' questions by telling a story about a forgiving father, who represents God, and a rebellious son. "There was a man who had two sons. The younger one said to his father 'Father, give me my share of the estate.' So he divided his property between them." I do not have to go in to all the dirty details because I am sure you have heard the story before. Hearing is one thing, listening is another. In a nutshell—this son blew it—big time. Hmmm. This reminds me of myself, and quite possibly a few of my new closest and dearest shamed and broken girlfriends.

To fully help you understand just how shameful this young man behaved, allow me to throw some interesting factoids into the mix. First, this "unrighteous" dude should never have asked for his inheritance in the first place. Instead, his father should have chosen when and where to give out his goods. This was Jewish tradition. Secondly, this sinful son's responsibility was to care for his parents, not the other way around. Finally, when he hit his famine-fraught fate, he took the most despicable job possible for a Jewish man—caring for hogs. According to Jewish law, pigs were considered unclean. The Pharisees would have absolutely flipped out.

In spite of all his shortcomings, his father did the unthinkable upon his reluctant return. He ran to him. In the New Testament, running in public was undignified. Not only did he run, but he lavished him with gifts. "But the father said to his servants, 'Quick! Bring the best robe and put it on him. Put a ring on his finger and sandals on his feet. Bring the fattened calf and kill it. Let's have a feast and celebrate. For this son of mine was dead and is alive again; he was lost and is found.' So they began to celebrate" (Luke 15:22-25).

My parents often question their reaction to my affair once it was exposed. What, if anything, could they have done differently? My response to them is simple, "Nothing. You loved me unconditionally, and that is all I really needed." That night, they ran to me. They did not judge me. They just loved me—something God had been doing all along.

Finally, understand your role in receiving forgiveness. As a once lost soul myself, I love the parable of the lost son. Have you ever noticed that the father forgave his son before he had even confessed his sin (Luke 15:20)? In the same way, our loving and merciful heavenly Father provided for our forgiveness, long before any of us could even ask. "In him we have redemption through his blood, the forgiveness of sins, in accordance with the riches of God's grace" (Ephesians 1:7). Frankly, forgiveness is in the blood; nothing but the blood.

More than that, God's Word tells us, "If we confess our sins, he is faithful and just and will forgive us our sins and purify us from all unrighteousness" (1 John 1:9). The Greek word for confess means "to agree with." How are you on agreeing with God?

Keep in mind there is more than one kind of forgiveness. When we trust Christ as our Savior, our sin-debt is cancelled—we begin a new relationship with God and have eternal security. But in order to maintain fellowship with God we have the responsibility to confess sins committed in our daily lives and receive forgiveness for them (1 John 1:9). Keep in mind, our eternal security does not translate in to an eternal sinning. Remind me, what did I say in Chapter 7 was a necessary step to get well? Oh, that is right—stop sinning. Period.

Despite shaming his family, the prodigal son never lost his "son-ship." You and I, as shamed and broken daughters, have never lost our "daughter-ship." It is when we choose not to return home to our Father that our fellowship is finished. If you continue to carry your own "claim to shame" of sexual sin everywhere you go, I

YOU AND I, AS SHAMED AND BROKEN DAUGHTERS, HAVE NEVER LOST OUR "DAUGHTER-SHIP."

invite you to carry it to the Lord through this simple prayer:

"Dear God, by faith in the testimony of Jesus, I accept You as my loving heavenly Father—not an angry, unforgiving father. Your love is unlimited, and You are eager to restore fellowship with me, Your child. Expose the errors of my thinking, and fill me with the truth, for I know that in discovering the truth, I will be set free. Amen."

"Set free." It is for freedom that Christ set us free. Just as Christ poured himself out on the cross for our sins, we too can pour ourselves out for Him in an unashamed act of love. We can choose to believe in His forgiveness—to be set free. One woman in the Bible "who lived a sinful life" modeled this faith step to us in the form of an alabaster jar.

When one of the Pharisees invited Jesus to have dinner with him, he went to the Pharisee's house and reclined at the table. A woman in that town who lived a (sexual) sinful life learned that Jesus was eating at the Pharisee's house, she came there with an alabaster jar of perfume. As she stood behind him at his feet weeping, she began to wet his feet with her tears. Then she wiped them with her hair, kissed them and poured perfume on them. (Luke 7:36-38)

Just like you and me, that jar was probably laced with cracks of sexual shame. This sinful woman lavished tears, expensive perfume, and kisses on Jesus—all from a state of cracked-open brokenness. She was condemned by the religious, yet forgiven by a Savior.

In contrast, Simon, Jesus' Pharisee "host without the most," neglected to wash His feet, anoint His head or even offer a kiss of greeting. Jesus rebukes the man. "Do you see this woman? I came into your house. You did not give me any water for my feet, but she wet my feet with her tears and wiped them with her hair. You did not give me a kiss, but this woman, from the time I entered, has not stopped kissing my feet. You did not put oil on my head, but she has poured perfume on my feet. Therefore, I tell you, her many sins have been forgiven—as her great love has shown. But whoever has been forgiven little loves little" (Luke 7:44-47).

In this story, it is the grateful prostitute and not the religious leader whose sins were forgiven. Although God's grace through faith is what saves us and not acts of love or generosity, this woman's act demonstrated her true faith, and Jesus honored her. Jesus forgave her. Jesus forgave them all.

Jesus forgives you and me too. Jesus' love language to us is forgiveness and our love language to him is faith. Pure and simple. Your faith, my stainless sister, is what makes you fluent.

Reflections at the Well

Based on your relationship with your earthly father, how do you view God?

Considering the biblical example of the prodigal son, how does God demonstrate His love for you as a broken and shamed woman?

What is your role in receiving forgiveness?

End your time at the Well by, if you have not already, sincerely praying the "forgiveness prayer" shared in this chapter.

Chapter 10

CHICKEN SOUPY

Although we live in the world, we do not wage war as the world does.
(2 Corinthians 10:3)

I am sick. No, for real this time. As I type this chapter, I am literally lying in bed, flanked on either side by a Dachshund and Chihuahua, with a fever, stuffy nose, cough, aches, and pains. Woe is me! All of a sudden, in the mist of medication, I am reminded of a "get well" card my sister once received from her childhood best friend, "Sorry you are feeling a little droopy. All you need is some chicken soupy." I am thinking the Campbell Soup Company used this card as a shameful plug.

Why is it that when we are "sick" everyone seems to have a solution? You know what I am talking about. Somehow everyone you know instantly morphs into a medical expert. "Try a spoonful of cinnamon and honey. That should do the trick," or "You know what you need? You need some Emergen C." This is exactly what happened to me when my affair was exposed. Immediately, friends and family began offering their own "home-grown" homeopathic solutions.

Just like physical illness, the "germs" of childhood abuse, rape, adultery, and sin in general, if left untreated, will eat away at our individual immunity. Even the most "Christian" of Christians can find themselves susceptible to all sorts of germ-infested illnesses such as anxiety disorders, depression, eating disorders, dissociative disorders, and personality disorders.

I have found that when it comes to treating these illnesses, there are two schools of thought. Medical experts say it is chemical. Christians say it is spiritual. I say it is both.

Hear me out on this one. Just this past weekend, I had "the talk" with my parents. When I say "the talk," I mean the long-avoided-but-necessary conversation about my own recently-discovered reality of a childhood "germed" by sexual abuse.

For months now, I have literally talked myself in and out of telling the truth—the truth as I saw it through the eyes of a freckle-faced, pig-tailed little girl. This truth of childhood sexual abuse, exposed openly and honestly in Chapter 1, was a truth that I had not yet addressed with my parents. The truth was I was avoiding it. Although I knew sharing the truth was essential, not only for my own healing and restoration but for the healing and restoration of others, I continued to justify leaving it out. It was just so shameful.

"I know what you are asking of me, God, but I cannot hurt my family again. They have already been through so much. Maybe what I experienced was not really sexual abuse. Maybe I should just leave this information out." Leave it out? What happened to the truth setting me free? Without "the talk," I would continue to be bound in shameful shackles. Before I could even think to publish this book, and to avoid shaming my family anymore, I would have to have "the talk." But how?

If you ever question the sovereignty of the Lord, think back to the last time something unexplainable happened. We call them miracles. Miracles like that twenty-dollar bill showing up in your pocket just when you needed it. Miracles like that test you did not study for being rescheduled (yes, I live in a college town). Miracles like that really hard conversation with your parents about your own childhood sexual abuse. A miracle happened to me this past Saturday.

While casually watching the Aggie football game on TV with my parents in their living room, the unexplainable happened. We had "the talk." Without a plan to even do so, I shared the truth, as I saw it, with my parents. What happened next was even more of a miracle. Not only was I set free from my own shame of childhood sexual abuse, but my dad experienced the beginning of freedom for himself.

FOR THE FIRST TIME IN HIS LIFE, MY DAD SHARED A MOMENT IN HIS CHILDHOOD THAT SHAMED HIM.

For the first time in his life, my dad shared a moment in his childhood that shamed him.

Spiritual Germs

Why did it take my dad so long to share his childhood wound? My guess is that shame played a big role in keeping him silent. Since my affair, the sinful "scales" that once covered my own eyes have been removed to discern the brokenness in others. For some time, I had sensed the brokenness in my dad. Moments of quiet reflection coupled with bouts of depression had presented themselves as "symptoms" in my dad's diagnosis. My dad, like so many, was suffering from a serious case of "shameitis"—a disease brought on by both chemical (how God created him) and spiritual (how others created him) germs. Allow me to explain.

Just like me, my dad developed a wrong pattern of thinking at a young age because of a traumatic event that shamed him. This wrong pattern of thinking justified a wrong behavior. This wrong behavior caused my dad to erect his own stronghold of shame, which only perpetuated his pain by keeping the trauma locked in and God locked out.

The key word in the above paragraph is **stronghold**. Liberty Savad explains it best in her book *Shattering Your Strongholds* (which I highly recommend), "A stronghold is a 'sickness' that someone uses to fortify and defend a personal belief, idea or opinion against outside opposition. If you have believed and bought into a lie, you will automatically fight to protect that belief. The lie usually comes in the form of an 'un-word.'" For example, I am unclean, unloved, unwanted, unsuccessful, and unworthy. Sound familiar? Who told you that? Perhaps Satan? If you have decided these lies are truth, you will erect a stronghold to defend your right to believe it. Repeated attempts by those around you to convince you it is a lie will be viewed as attacks, causing you to reinforce its protective stronghold.

This is what happens through the spiritual "germination" of generational sin.

When God gave the Ten Commandments to Moses, He clearly stated that He was a jealous God, "punishing the children for the sin of the parents to the third and fourth generations" (Exodus 20:5). This Scripture slides the shame and brokenness of sexual sin under a spiritual microscope, revealing its true origin. Unrepentant sin, whether sexual or otherwise, is likely to "poison" generation

THE ANTIDOTE TO THIS DISEASE-CAUSING POISON IS SPIRITUAL WARFARE.

after generation, causing strongholds to be erected left and right.

The antidote to this disease-causing poison is spiritual warfare.

"Although we live in the world, we do not wage war as the world does. The weapons we fight with are not the weapons of the world. On the contrary, they have divine power to demolish strongholds. We demolish arguments and every pretention that sets itself up against the knowledge of God, and we take every thought captive to make it obedient to Christ" (2 Corinthians 10:3-5). Notice this Scripture says, "we." One of the keys to my restoration was soliciting "prayer warriors" to "stand in the gap" for me. You cannot fight this battle on your own. Who can you ask to pray for you?

Generational sin is a spiritual battle fought through the prayers of binding and loosing. This is how you "take every thought captive." "Truly I tell you, whatever you bind on earth will be bound in heaven, and whatever you loose on earth will be loosed in heaven" (Matthew 18:18). So what does that mean—binding and loosing? Binding refers to "joining" your will, your thoughts, and your life to the will of God. Loosing, on the other hand, refers to "destroying" the ties Satan has over your will, your thoughts, and your life. Keep in mind, some believers see binding and loosing as the opposite—binding up the enemy and loosing his hold on you. Either way, the idea is prayer warfare through claiming Scripture. When it comes to destroying the strongholds of generational sin, the "training wheels" prayer below, written by Liberty Savard, was a great place for me to start. I encourage you to read it out loud daily until you find a release from bondage in your own spirit.

Binding and Loosing Prayer

"Lord, I am standing on the truth of your Word. You said you would give me the keys to the kingdom, that whatever I would bind on earth would be bound in heaven and whatever I loose on earth would be loosed in heaven. Right now, in the name of Jesus Christ, I bind my will to the will of God, that

I will be constantly aware of His will and purposes for my life. I bind myself to the truth of God that I will not be deceived by the many subtle deceptions of the world and the devil.

I bind myself to the blood of Jesus that I will never take it for granted. I want to be constantly aware of its miracle-working power to restore and heal and keep me safe. I bind myself to the mind of Christ that I will be aware of how Jesus would have me think in every situation I come into this day. I do not want to react out of my own human, carnal thoughts when situations arise suddenly, I want to think and act as Jesus would have me act. I bind my feet to paths of righteousness that my steps will be steady and true all day long. I bind myself to the work of the cross in my life so that I will continue to die daily to my own selfish desires and motivations and be more like Him.

I repent of every wrong desire, attitude, and pattern of thinking I have had. Forgive me, Lord, for holding onto wrong ideas, desires, behaviors and habits. I renounce and reject these things. In the name of Jesus Christ, I loose every wrong attitude, pattern of thinking, belief, idea, desire, behavior, and habit I have ever learned. I loose the strongholds around them that would keep me from being completely surrendered to the will of God for my life. I loose all doubt and confusion from myself.

I have bound myself to the mind of Christ and I loose every wrong thought and evil imagination that will keep me from being in sweet unity with Him. I bind and loose these things in the name of Jesus Christ, who has given me the keys to do so. Thank you, Lord, for the truth."

Chemical Germs

When it came to my complete healing and restoration, it was necessary for me to treat not only the spiritual symptoms of my sexual sin through the warfare prayers of myself and others, but also the chemical symptoms of the illnesses innate in my body. I have found that this is one of the most controversial criticisms in Christianity. Many Christians believe the lie that "if you were just more Christian, you would not be depressed and anxious—you would not have a mental illness. You are not praying and believing enough. You cannot be a Christian and be depressed at the same time." Oh yes you can! This deceptive school of thought only shames the sinner more, halting any hope of healing.

I thank God for my Christ-believing family physician and therapist who have spoken truth over this debate in my own life time and time again. If you struggle with depression and anxiety, or any other mental illness (which is very common in the lives of those shamed and broken by sin), there is a very good chance that it is a chemical imbalance in your body. It is how God created you. The only way to treat a chemical imbalance is through medication.

I began taking anti-depressants shortly after my affair was exposed. The truth was, if I really took an honest look at my childhood, depression was there from the beginning. I believe that this depression came from both spiritual generational sin and the chemical DNA of my family tree. For me, treating the symptoms of depression with proper medication was necessary before my mind could even be clear enough to "journey

I NEEDED TO BE "IN BAL-ANCE" CHEMICALLY BEFORE I COULD BE WELL "SPIRITUALLY."

back." Depression "fogs" your thoughts and drains your energy. I needed to be "in balance" chemically before I could be well "spiritually." The spiritual battle of generational sin would require every ounce of my energy.

If you suspect that your struggle with mental illness is chemical, I urge you to seek the wisdom and advice of a Christian physician. If he or she suggests medication, be humble enough to accept their diagnosis. Most of all, be patient. Finding the right "mix" of medication may take months. Be open to seeing a licensed therapist, if that is what your physician recommends. It is important to not "play doctor" by choosing, on your own, when you are "well enough" to stop medicating. I can remember the one and only time I "played doctor" with my own medication.

Some "Christian" had shamed me over the fact that I was still treating my depression with medication. "Why are you still taking medication?" my accuser asked. "If you believed God for healing, you would stop taking your meds."

"She is right," I thought. "God has healed me. I do not need meds anymore." So, I stopped "cold turkey" taking my medication. Huge mistake. Within twenty-four hours, I was experiencing the worst of withdrawal symptoms. I immediately made an appointment with my PA. As I cried in her office over the shameful fact that I was not "well enough" yet, she lovingly spoke truth over me.

"Traci, I was born with an auto-immune deficiency," she explained. "I used to be angry with God for making me this way. Why couldn't I just be healthy? But then I decided that I could use my illness to help others. That is why I decided to become a PA. For some reason, God created you with a chemical imbalance that manifests itself in depression. It does not make you any less of a Christian. God created you for His good purposes. He created the scientists who created the medication to treat you. Just like me, you can use your illness for good."

The Great Physician is speaking the same truth in your life. His God-sized greeting card says to you, "Sorry you are feeling a little droopy, all you need is some of My spirit-filled soupy." He promises to "restore to you the years that the locust hath eaten...And ye shall eat in plenty, and be satisfied, and praise the name of the Lord your God, that hath dealt wondrously with you; and my people shall never be ashamed" (Joel 2:25-26 KJV). That is why our God is so "M'm M'm good."

Reflections at the Well

What "un-words" have perpetuated the stronghold lies in your life?

What is the difference between binding and loosing? Who could you ask to "stand in the gap" for you?

Have you ever considered the "chemical" side of your illness? Who could you contact for professional help in this treatment?

End your time at the Well by praying aloud the "binding and loosing" prayer shared in this chapter.

Chapter 11

BACK TO THE FUTURE

Train a child in the way he should go, and when
he is old he will not turn from it. (Proverbs 22:6)

This year is a pinnacle year for the Smith family. Our oldest son, Arrott (pronounced "Carrot" without the "C") is graduating from high school. Our first graduate. You know what they say, you will never forget your first—first graduate that is.

Not only is it a year of firsts, but it is also a year of lasts. One moment while I grab my box of tissues. In August came his last first day of high school. September brought his last first high school football game. This month, the month of October, we are preparing for his last first high school homecoming dance as a senior. Sniffle. Sniffle. In fact, I just received the official "mom homecoming game plan" email from the lead homecoming game plan mom (or the LHGPM). This is really happening.

At the risk of sounding cliché, where did the time go? Seems like only yesterday that I was awakened from a deeply sedated sleep at Houston's Methodist Hospital to birth and meet my firstborn for the first time. He was absolutely perfect, every single inch of him. He had my heart from the get go. As a brand new mom, I can vividly remember crawling out of bed in the middle of the night, peering into his bassinet, and literally bawling because I was afraid "he would never know how much I love him."

Of course, we did all the things "normal" parents of firstborns do. We documented and photographed every single breath and moment of his little life. We even have a photograph of his grandmother holding him in one arm and, with her other hand, holding his long white "garland" of Diaper Genie "poop" bags (the things we do). What a proud moment!

Arrott was my entire world. I would protect him at every cost, even to the point of giving my husband the silent treatment for an entire week. Allow me to explain. When Arrott was a newborn, we decided to take him on a little trip to Houston's Galleria Mall. It may have been a "little" trip, but this was no "little" mall. As doting parents, we paraded Arrott up and down the halls of the mall, being sure to pause for a moment for occasional onlookers who wished to gaze in awe at his splendor.

As we made our way up the mall escalator, my husband Brian chose to keep our slumbering son in his blue-checkered stroller so as to not awaken our "sleeping giant." Brian tilted the stroller onto its back wheels, and rolled on to the moving escalator. Just then, I saw my firstborn "perfect" son, Arrott, slide out of the escalator and land face down on one of its metal steps. You could have thought the earth came to a screeching halt. My "protective mom" instinct reared its ugly head.

Like some kind of sumo wrestler/cheetah, I shoved and leapt my way up the escalator steps just in time to save my swaddled son from the grinding teeth of the top escalator stair. Brian, who assumed that Arrott was just one of our mall pilgrimage packages, had no idea what happened. I can distinctly remember screaming at him (with steam most likely spewing out of my ears). He was to "never touch our son again—ever." Okay, so I was a little extreme. But, he **was** my firstborn, and I would do anything to protect him.

Those strict stipulations were, of course, tossed out the window that very same night when diaper-changing time came. Let me reassure you, my protective instincts have definitely become more lax. I am sure that Arrott is grateful to not be wearing a protective layer of "bubble wrap" from head to toe. At some point and time, I had to allow my son to grow up—to grow in to his confident independence. Now, I find myself wishing that I could go back, just to hold my oldest in my arms one more time. Parenting requires an astronomical amount of trust. We train them up just to let them go.

"Start children off on the way they should go, and even when they are old they will not turn from it" (Proverbs 22:6). This Scripture, written with the end in mind, gives specific instructions to parents. The King James Version of this verse instructs the parent to "train up a child in the way he should go: and when he is old, he will not depart from it." Train up. Start off.

TO MOVE FORWARD INTO THE FUTURE GOD HAS FOR US, WE MUST GO BACK.

What was your "start off" like? How were you "trained up"? Whether it was good or bad, pretty or ugly, hurtful or happy, I believe that our past absolutely shapes or "trains" our future. To move forward into the future God has for us, we must go back. Restoration requires going back to the future.

Write a Letter

Believe me, no one wanted to know "why" I chose to have an affair more than I did. It was so "out of character," so much so that it really had me "shame struck." Before my affair, I, too, sat in a stadium of "saintly" judgment with other local modern-day Pharisees (many are still sitting in those seats at our local high school football games, "graciously" giving our family the cold shoulder as we pass by). "How could she do that? I would **never** do what she did!" I am sure they are chomping at the bit to read this adulterous version of the Academy-Award winning *The Help* (and to be honest, I cannot wait for them to read it).

If they only knew the truth. The truth was and the truth is, that each and every one of us has a messy past—a messy past that, even at birth, was imposed upon us. With any luck, we will humble ourselves enough to "go there" and deal with source of our sin—our past. I was one of the "lucky" ones.

During my journey back, I was fortunate to participate in an eternity-changing Bible Study titled *The Ultimate Journey* (or Christ Life). I often laugh about the first time I met my fellow "journeyers" at our first Christ Life session. One by one, we went around the table introducing ourselves, sharing not only our names, but why we were there. One participant shared that she did not know why she was there. Another shared just her name. And then there was me.

"I am here because I had an affair, and I want to know why." Um okay. Talk about an impressionable first impression. No sense in "sugar coating" it, I was there to take care of business. Phase I of *The Ultimate Journey* focuses on "unpacking self-deception"—deception that begins at birth. At the conclusion of our first session video, we were asked to write an "Ally" letter from the Adult Us to the Child Us. Boy, do I wish we were sitting face to face right now. I can only imagine your puzzled facial expression, marked with a mindset of "Okay, this is getting weird now." Listen, I hear ya, sister. I thought the exact same thing.

Reluctantly, I assumed a childlike position on the cold linoleum floor of our church classroom. Then, with pen in hand, I began writing. "Dear Little Traci." The tears came from nowhere, or later I would learn, somewhere down deep. With a rage and level of deep-rooted pain I was not aware of, I began writing down all the ways that I felt wounded by my family and others as a young child. I closed the letter with two sentences, "I accept you for who you are. You have value and worth. Love, Big Traci." Next, I wrote a letter back to the Adult Me from the Child Me, using my non-dominant hand. The letter, though awkward, began with these two insightful sentences, "Do you really think I deserve to be loved? How could anyone love me?" I realized at that moment this was serious soul-sifting stuff.

As children, you and I both needed an "Adult Ally" to "go to bat" for us. This Adult Ally was supposed to be someone you could express your feelings, thoughts, wants, and needs to. It should have been someone you could confide in who would bless you, nurture you, and affirm you. Too often, this is not the case. Instead, our

> AS CHILDREN, YOU AND I BOTH NEEDED AN "ADULT ALLY" TO "GO TO BAT" FOR US.

parents or caregivers create more harm than good in our lives. No blame is placed on them directly, because they most likely received this same "love" from their parents or caregivers, proving that it is not necessarily what is taught, but rather what is caught, that impacts our future.

Whether for good or bad, we are "trained" to see ourselves through lie-laced lenses. To make matters worse, we "buy in" to those lies, and we eventually become our worst enemies. You learned to see yourself the way that others saw you. This "training up" has resulted in your inability to love yourself and receive the love God has for you. Of course, this often is because you are shamed over things done to you or things you have personally done. Here is a truth bomb for you courtesy of *The Ultimate Journey*: "Guilt is feeling bad about something you do whereas shame is feeling bad about who you are." In the end, we live in constant conflict.

This conflict can only be resolved when the adult "you" chooses to side with God on your behalf—you become the "Adult Ally" you never had.

Week by week, my new *Ultimate Journey* "freedom family" dealt with our "junk"—from birth to early childhood to elementary school to middle school to high school to our young adult years to our adult years. Openly and unashamedly, through a series of letter writing from Adult to Child, from Child to Adult, and so on, we were being restored.

10 Steps to Ally

So how do you and I become our own ally? Here are some simple steps that I learned via letter writing through *The Ultimate Journey*:

1. **Love**, accept, and approve of the child you used to be. Example: "You are lovable and totally acceptable as far as I am concerned. I am so proud of you."

2. **Affirm** the child with words that encourage, empower, and lift up. Example: "In all the world there is not another one like you. No one could ever take your place. You have everything it takes to have a wonderful and successful life."

3. **Understand** that not everything that happened was your fault. So now you can stop blaming, hating, or neglecting the child you used to be. Example: "That was not your fault. You are not bad. What was done to you was bad, but that does not make you bad or shameful. You are innocent and lovable."

4. **Validate** all the feelings that are expressed as you hear the depths of the child's heart. Remember: feelings are for feeling, not for fixing. Example: "It is okay to be mad about that. Being mad is not wrong. What was said to you was wrong and hurtful."

5. **Comfort** and embrace the child. Example: "I want you to know that it is okay for you to cry and to express emotions. I will listen to you and be here for you and do whatever I can to help you. I am so sorry that happened to you. I am here for you now."

6. **Correct** the false beliefs that the child accepted as truth which were actually lies. Example: "I know you believed that you are responsible for other people's feelings and reactions. The truth is that other people need to deal with their own feelings and reactions. You are only responsible for what you feel and do in light of your relationship with God."

7. **Forgive** the child completely wherever forgiveness is needed. Example: "That was a bad choice you made, but I understand why you made it. We all make mistakes. God forgives you and I forgive you."

8. **Protect** the child by no longer allowing others to treat you in a way that is hurtful or damaging. "I am here to guard your heart. I will only let the truth come in. No matter what other people do or do not do, I will protect you and be here for you."

9. **Give** the child whatever he or she needs because you know the child's needs are important. Example: "It is okay for you to have needs. Your needs are very important to me. I will see to it that you get everything you need."

10. **Take** ownership of the care of this child from now on so that you will not ever again have to feel neglected or abandoned. "I am here for you now. Whatever you are going through, we are going through together. I am going to be here to give you a voice. I will listen to you. I will comfort you. I will see that your needs get met. I will tell you the truth. Together we are going to make it."

"Above all else, guard your heart for it is the wellspring of life" (Proverbs 4:23). You, too, have the opportunity to give yourself what you never received as a child—an ally. All it takes is a pen, piece of paper, and a willingness to track back to your past for your future. I double dog dare you to write that first letter. Allow me to help you with your first three words. "Dear Little Me."

Reflections at the Well

What was your "start off" like? How were you "trained up"?

Write a letter from the Adult You to the Child You. Then, write a reply letter from the Child You to the Adult You using your non-dominant hand. What "soul wounds" were exposed through these letters?

Which of the "10 Steps to Ally" did you most need as a child?

End your time at the Well by "allying" yourself aloud using one of the "10 Steps to Ally."

Chapter 12

THE LABEL MAKER

It is for freedom that Christ set us free. Stand firm, then, and do not let yourselves be burdened again by a yoke of slavery. (Galatians 5:1)

I am often asked how my husband and I came up with our "unique" children's first names. Because our last name is "Smith," and my husband is "Brian Smith" (who by the way is on the "no fly list" due to his fugitive status—rest assured, my husband is **not that** "Brian Smith"), Brian was adamant that his boys **not** have "common" first names. And, we delivered (no pun intended).

Our firstborn, Arrott (pronounced "Carrot" without the "C") is named after Brian's grandmother on his father's side. Brayson, our middle "miracle," is a combination of both our first names—"Brian" and "Traci" with "son" on the end. Then there is our "bonus" child—Caden.

I will never forget the day that I found out I was pregnant with Caden. It was September 12, 2001, the day after "911." Just the day before, I had watched in disgust and disbelief as terrorists murdered more than 3,000 innocent Americans with commercial airplanes turned weapons. Like most Americans, I felt violated and afraid. Non-stop footage of desperate people jumping to their death from the World Trade Center was almost more than I could bear. I cried and clung to my two toddler boys. I was an emotional wreck.

For weeks, I had not been feeling quite right. So when a girlfriend suggested that I might be pregnant, I laughed it off as "post 911" partum. With so many unanswered questions about Brayson's difficult birth, pregnancy was not even on the radar for the Smith family. Because Brayson was nearly delivered stillborn, I was terrified that a third child would not survive. One positive pregnancy test later, and I was frantically on the phone with my know-it-all girlfriend, "Oh (insert expletive here)! I am pregnant!" After her reassuring "I told you so," I called Brian in tears to announce the questionable "good news."

Later that afternoon, another girlfriend of mine stopped by to pray with me. Word had already circulated through the church like "breaking news" with the headline reading: "Smiths Pregnant Again!" She knew that I was less than thrilled at the possibility of another life-or-death pregnancy experience. With a peaceful reassurance, she looked me square in the eye and said, "Traci, this child will be a child of joy." Through the Lord she claimed it, and, therefore, I believed it.

When it came time to choose a baby name, Brian and I were convinced that, first and foremost, this child's name had to start with the letter "C" (to stick with the already established alphabetical order theme of Arrott and Brayson). For some reason, the name "Caden" continued to pop up at the top of our list. So, when we discovered that "Caden" literally meant "one of joy" it was a "Dunn" deal ("Dunn" would have been our fourth child's name, had we had one, to make a very clear point, we were done)!

The funny thing was that Caden was anything but joy-filled during his first two months of life. Saving the best for last, Caden was our one and only child to suffer from colic, which meant that he screamed twenty-four hours a day non-stop. At the risk of being reported to Child Protective Services, I humbly confess placing Caden on several occasions, in his car seat, out on the side porch of our small three bedroom duplex, then closing the door behind him, so he could cry his little heart out. Do not worry, the yard was fenced in and he had plenty of shade (like that makes it any better). "One of joy"—right. God sure did have a great sense of humor.

Fast forward twelve years later. Caden is the happiest kid you will ever meet. He is easy going, laid back, smiles all the time, rarely complains, and has the biggest servant's heart. Those who meet him for the first time often ask, "Is he always this happy?" Boy, if they only knew! He truly is living up to his God-ordained given name.

What if we had not named Caden, "Caden?" What if we had chosen a different name? A name that meant, "I gave birth to him and he screamed." Sounds like a story I once read in the Bible—a story about a man named "Jabez." Jabez was cursed from the get go. "Jabez was more honorable than his brothers. His mother had named him Jabez, saying, 'I gave birth to him in pain'"

NEGATIVE LABELS LIKE THIS TEND TO STICK TO US LIKE SUPERGLUE.

(1 Chronicles 4:9). Do not get me wrong, childbirth can be painful. But who in their right mind would label a child in such a way? Jabez carried with him, from birth, the label of "pain." Negative labels like this tend to stick to us like superglue.

Jabez is not the only one. We all have them. If we dare track back to our past (which is discussed in the previous chapter), we would discover "labels of lies" that have been stamped out and stuck on us since birth. Although they appear invisible to the human eye, they are so very visible in our hearts and minds. Reminds me of a popular song out today titled *Shake It Off* by Taylor Swift. In the song, the often scrutinized Swift's solution to the "haters" and those who label her with lies is simple—just shake it off. Wouldn't it be nice if we could simply "shake off" the labels of lies spoken over us? Oh, if it were only that easy!

Instead, our brains are programmed at birth, like mini "label makers," to process data in this way: when painful memories and wrong thoughts are inputted, the "label maker" interprets a distorted view of God, ourselves, and others. The output, or labels created, are labels of addiction and dysfunction. On the other hand, when healed memories and truthful thinking are inputted, we live with a true view of God, ourselves, and others that can only lead to freedom and wholeness. These truth labels are few and far between, but they are the ones that really matter.

As broken and shame-labeled women, how do we reprogram ourselves to "print out" the correct and truthful labels about ourselves instead of the false labels of lies? I suggest doing what I did—hook your life up to a God-Sized Lie Detector.

The God-Sized Lie Detector

Critical on my journey back, the Lie Detector allowed me to painfully and arduously dissect my past through the truthful lenses of an Almighty God. In each stage of my life (from birth to adulthood), I recalled events or situations that left imprints, or soul wounds, labeling who I am today. In a chart, I listed the event or situation (what happened or did not happen that wounded me), followed by my feelings about that event or situation (what emotions did I feel as a result), followed by the lies created from that event or situation (what did I come to believe about myself) and ending with the truth about that event or situation (what is God's truth that I need to side with).

For example, as a little girl, my perception was that I always had to look perfect—everything had to match. Because I could never look perfect enough, I always felt "less than" and "unworthy" of love. I believed the lie that love was based on outward appearances—that how I looked on the outside was more important than who I was on the inside. But God's truth tells me that "the Lord looks at the heart" (1 Samuel 16:7). Bam! Take that Lie Detector!

One by one, the labels of lies from my past were "ripped" from my soul and the truth of who I am in Christ took their place. I would recall the incident, uncover the feelings associated with that incident (most likely translated in the form of an "un" word), call the lie for what it was, and replace the lie with God's truth. Freedom came each time I overcame the lies with God's truth. "It is for freedom that Christ set us free. Stand firm, then, and do not let yourselves be burdened again by a yoke of slavery" (Galatians 5:1).

Notice that this Scripture says, "Stand firm, then, and do not let yourselves be burdened again by a yoke of slavery." This means, once free always free! But, how is that possible? It seems like every time I have victory, the devil recounts another "lie" through "trigger moments." Trigger

WE EITHER CHOOSE TO BELIEVE THE LIE, OR WE REPLACE THE LIE WITH GOD'S TRUTH.

moments are those moments when you are pushed to your absolute limits or "margins," (margins meaning the difference between what you have in your life and what you need in your life), and thus reality becomes skewed. At that moment, you and I have a choice to make. We either choose to believe the lie, or we replace the lie with God's truth.

Insert "victory verses" right here. It is essential, if not absolutely critical, that you and I have a list of "Victory Verses" to call forth as truth in our lives when in the thick of a trigger moment battle. This is why the Lie Detector Chart is so important. It forces you and me into God's space to, not only hear, but actually listen to and learn from His truth about every lie we have ever come to own. I have included some examples of these verses below in a list that has been a "life line" to me. Each verse listed is followed by a summarized truth about who we are in Christ. I encourage you to not only make a copy and hang it on your bathroom mirror, but actually dive in to God's Word to discover the truth of who you really are. Read a truth aloud each time you stand in front of the mirror. Repeat that truth while looking yourself straight in the eyes. Begin with this truth, **you** are beautiful.

The Truth About Who I Am in Christ

I am accepted...
John 1:12–*I am God's child.*
John 15:15–*I am a friend of Jesus Christ.*
Romans 5:1–*I have been justified.*
1 Corinthians 6:17–*I am united with the Lord, and I am one with Him in spirit.*
1 Corinthians 6:19-20–*I have been bought with a price and I belong to God.*
1 Corinthians 12:27–*I am a member of Christ's body.*
Ephesians 1:3-8–*I have been chosen by God and adopted as His child.*
Colossians 1:13-14–*I have been redeemed and forgiven of all my sins.*
Colossians 2:9-10–*I am complete in Christ.*
Hebrews 4:14-16–*I have direct access to the throne of grace through Jesus Christ.*

I am secure...

Romans 8:1-2–*I am free from condemnation.*

Romans 8:28–*I am assured that God works for my good in all circumstances.*

Romans 8:31-39–*I am free from any condemnation and I cannot be separated from the love of God.*

2 Corinthians 1:21-22–*I have been established, anointed and sealed by God.*

Colossians 3:1-4–*I am hidden with Christ in God.*

Philippians 1:6–*I am confident that God will complete the good work He started in me.*

Philippians 3:20–*I am a citizen of heaven.*

2 Timothy 1:7–*I have not been given a spirit of fear but of power, love, and a sound mind.*

1 John 5:18–*I am born of God and the evil one cannot touch me.*

I am significant...

John 15:5–*I am a brand of Jesus Christ, the true vine, and a channel of His life.*

John 15:16–*I have been chosen and appointed to bear fruit.*

1 Corinthians 3:16–*I am God's temple.*

2 Corinthians 5:17-21–*I am a minister of reconciliation for God.*

Ephesians 2:6–*I am seated with Jesus Christ in the heavenly realm.*

Ephesians 2:10–*I am God's workmanship.*

Ephesians 3:12–*I may approach God with freedom and confidence.*

Philippians 4:13–*I can do all things through Christ who strengthens me.*

At a business women's retreat I recently hosted, I led a group of twenty women through their own Lie Detector Test based on the film *Seven Days in Utopia*. When asked if anyone would unashamedly share a "lie" spoken over them, one by one, women stood and shared their lies through painful tears. Once they owned that lie openly, I asked them to write all their lies down on a lime green "sticky note." Each broken woman was then asked to "unstick" that lie, carry it to the front of the room and bury it in a container of dirt, just as I did that fateful day over Spring Break in Utopia, Texas. Once the lie was buried, they were to move on and "unearth" a truth about themselves in the form of a buried golf ball. Each golf ball had the letters SFT (See His Face, Feel His presence; Trust His love) written on them, as well as one of the above Bible verses. As the Lord would have it, each Bible verse was exactly what each women needed to fight her particular lie.

Freedom happened that day. That same freedom is available to you. "It is for freedom that Christ set us free. Stand firm, then, and do not let yourselves be burdened again by a yoke of slavery" (Galatians 5:1). Allow His God-Sized Label Maker to stick truth on your soul-wounded heart today. Click. Click. Click. Print. Truth.

Reflections at the Well

What "lie labels" have been stuck on you for far too long?

On a sheet of paper, create a Lie Detector chart with the following column titles: Event/Situation (What happened/did not happen that wounded me); Feeling (What emotions did I feel as a result?); Lie (What did I come to believe about myself?); and Truth (What is God's truth that I need to side with?) Use this chart to detect lies in your early childhood years.

Which of the "Victory Verses" do you most need to memorize and why?

End your time at the Well by printing out the "Victory Verses" list shared in this chapter. Post this list on your bathroom mirror and commit to speaking one verse a day, out loud, while looking at yourself in the mirror. Begin to "own" the truth about who you are in Christ.

Chapter 13

THE ROAD TO RECONCILIATION

All of this is from God, who reconciled us to himself through Christ and gave us the ministry of reconciliation: that God was reconciling the world to himself in Christ, not counting men's sins against them. And he has committed to us the ministry of reconciliation. (2 Corinthians 5:18-19)

Life is a series of roads. Some roads lead to a dead end. Some roads send us in circles, and some simply usher us out. No matter the road, they all have one commonality—each road serves as a reminder. Last night, I traveled a road that reminded me of how far I have come, and how grateful I was for second chances.

For thirteen chapters now, you and I have journeyed this often rough and raw Restoration Road together. Just like any other "road trip," we have stopped at all sorts of "historical markers" along the way. Today, I want to take you back to one particular historical marker on my journey back—the Buried Lies Cemetery in Utopia, Texas. At the risk of sounding like the famous radio-commentator Paul Harvey, now you get to read "the rest of the story."

During the eight months prior to this historical cemetery "detour," Brian and I had consistently been attending a healing ministry called Divorce Care. Due to our hostility, animosity, and overall lack of civil communication unless through attorneys, we attended Divorce Care on separate nights—Brian on Wednesdays and me on Tuesdays. Divorce Care drives participants down an emotional restoration road with necessary stops at such destinations as Anger Avenue, Depression Drive, and Loneliness Lane. The final two sessions focus on two very significant markers in the life of a broken and bruised divorcee—forgiveness and reconciliation. Consider these the "dashes" on the road to restoration.

Forgiveness

I have heard it said that "unforgiveness toward another person is like drinking poison with the expectation that the other person dies." The consequences of unforgiveness are many including depression (which is anger turned inward), bitterness and negativity, hurt to those around you, and physical, spiritual and emotional sickness, and loneliness. Forgiveness, on the other hand, produces the fruit of freedom. When you and I truly forgive those who have wounded us, they no longer have power over us.

In order to move forward in our lives, whether separate or together, Brian and I had to come to our own historical marker at a destination called forgiveness. We had to choose to forgive each other's adulterous acts—mine with another man and his with the church.

Forgiveness is a decision, not a feeling. When we forgive, it does not mean we minimize the offense, condone the other person's behavior, trust the other person again, or let the other person off the hook. Forgiveness is not forgetting. Forgiveness is moving forward.

As I was burying my lies in that cemetery on that sunny Spring Break day, I was choosing to forgive Brian. It was an act of total obedience to a forgiving and loving God. "For if you forgive men when they sin against you, your heavenly Father will also forgive you. But if you do not forgive men their sins, your Father will not forgive your sins" (Matthew 6:14-15). In essence, I put the "poison" down, and picked the "peace" up.

FORGIVENESS IS NOT FORGETTING. FORGIVENESS IS MOVING FORWARD.

I love God's promise to believers when we live our lives according to His rules, "The Lord will make you the head, not the tail. If you pay attention to the commands of the Lord your God that I give you this day and carefully follow them, you will always be at the top, never at the bottom" (Deuteronomy 28:13). When we are brought to our knees in total surrender, He reciprocates with a radical rise. But how do we forgive?

The process of forgiving is simple and Scripture-based. First, we must ask God to forgive us through true repentance (Chapter 6), asking with the expectation of receiving rest through His forgiveness. "Come to me, all you who are weary and burdened, and I will give you rest" (Matthew 11:28). Second, we must transfer our hurts, habits and hang-ups to Him (Chapter 11). "Cast all your anxiety on him because he cares for you" (1 Peter 5:7). Finally, we must turn the other person over to God. "Do not say, 'I'll pay you back for this wrong!' Wait for the Lord, and he will deliver you" (Proverbs 20:22). You will know when you have truly forgiven the other person when you can allow God's love to flow through you toward that person.

Like a really bad car accident, my ruthless road trip down Adulterous Avenue wrecked relationships and raised roadblocks that may never be restored or removed. Not everyone will choose forgiveness. But my choice to forgive my husband gave me peace. "If it is possible, as far as it depends on you, live at peace with everyone. Do not take revenge, my friends, but leave room for God's wrath, for it is written: 'It is mine to avenge; I will repay,' says the Lord" (Romans 12:18-19). This path to peace would ultimately lead to the forgiveness of the Lord, my husband, and my children at an intersection called Reconciliation Road.

Reconciliation

Dr. Jim Talley, a Divorce Care contributor, says that, "You choose either reconciliation or the anger path. There is no other path to choose." At the very moment I chose to bury my anger with the devil's lies on that ranch-bound road trip, God's resurrection power was unleashed more than 273 miles away. As I pled with the Lord for our marriage, Brian attempted to paint away the memories of our once happy College Station home.

"YOU CHOOSE EITHER RECONCILIATION OR THE ANGER PATH. THERE IS NO OTHER PATH TO CHOOSE."

When our divorce was finalized, I moved to a rented house in the back of our neighborhood, so Brian and the boys could continue to live in our family home. Our efforts to keep some sort of normalcy for the boys proved to be too much financially, and Brian was forced to make the difficult decision of putting our house on the market. This decision, coupled with a recent relationship breakup between Brian and the woman he had been dating, resulted in new Spring Break plans of painting and preparing the house to sell.

As the Lord would have it, Brian just so "happened to" stumble upon photo after photo of the two of us during his emotional packing process. It was as if the Lord was dropping little hints of healing along the way. When the subtleties did not work, the Lord literally brought Brian to his knees on our concrete kitchen floor. In complete surrender, the Lord asked Brian to take three faith steps.

First, the Lord asked Brian to seek peace and reconciliation in our broken relationship (whatever that may look like). According to Divorce Care, reconciliation does not necessarily mean the restoration of a marriage. Rather, it could simply mean a harmonious friendship.

Second, the Lord reminded Brian that our boys needed both parents in their lives fulltime. We needed to learn to co-parent for the sake of our children.

Finally, the Lord declared that if there was any hope for reconciling our marriage, Brian would need to be willing to lay everything (our house, his job at the church, and what others may say or do) on the table. Everything.

So, in an act of total obedience, Brian said an immediate "yes" to the Lord and wrote a letter of reconciliation to his bride. This letter, which was purposefully placed on a stack of photo-filled framed memories in a plain cardboard moving box, anxiously awaited my post Spring Break drop off of the boys. The letter read,

"Traci, if you want to look through these or select others, let me know. **Please don't throw any away!** If you don't want them, I do. Looking through all of these this week has been good and bad. I don't want to throw anything away, including the possibility of being friends or more in the future.

I do not know how to fix anything and I don't know if it can be fixed, but all week I have thought about Divorce Care Video #12 on

Reconciliation. We will never know if there is a possibility for us with other people in our lives. This week alone was really good for me and was eye opening. I am going to commit to pursue **Christ only** and see what happens. I hope you had a good week with the boys and your family. Although I missed them terribly, I was glad they were with you and had a good time! Thanks for loving them! Brian"

Unfortunately, the unexpected "for sale" sign in our yard would keep me from reading Brian's love letter for several more weeks. When Brian offered to load some boxes in my car of "things" he had found in the house that belonged to me (including this letter), I refused to take them. "I don't want anything from you," I cried out to Brian from my car. In reality, I wanted everything. I just could not see past the "for sale" sign. To me, this sign might as well have been a "tombstone" marking the definitive death of our marriage.

AS BELIEVERS, GOD CALLS EACH ONE OF US TO A MINISTRY OF RECONCILIATION.

According to *Divorce Care*, there are three levels of reconciliation: basic civility, friendship, and relationship. During our eight months as a divorced couple, Brian and I had still not reached the "basic civility" level. Although reconciliation looked impossible, the reasons to reach some level of reconciliation were apparent to both of us. Not only was it what our children wanted and needed, but it was what the Lord had wanted all along. The moment we divorced was the moment we willfully removed ourselves from the center of God's will.

As believers, God calls each one of us to a ministry of reconciliation. Very few of us have the ears to listen. "All of this is from God, who reconciled us to himself through Christ and gave us the ministry of reconciliation:

that God was reconciling the world to himself in Christ, not counting men's sins against them. And he has committed to us the ministry of reconciliation" (2 Corinthians 5:18-19). In order to be reconciled, both parties must come to the intersection of Reconciliation Road at the same time.

Several weeks later, Brian showed up at the door step of my two-story rented house.

"We need to talk. It is about Arrott," Brian said in a serious tone. "May I come in?"

Without hesitation, I welcomed him into my living room. Brian began to share how he had read a concerning text message conversation between our oldest son and a young lady from his high school—the conversation was a solicitation from the young lady to our son for sex.

"I cannot handle this on my own," Brian continued. "You are his mother and I am his father. We need to address this as his parents."

We agreed to discuss the incident with Arrott at my home immediately after school. Surprisingly, the dialogue did not stop there. Although we had barely communicated verbally over our eight months as a divorced couple, the conversation flowed freely from issues regarding our children, our finances, and most importantly, our hearts. In a miraculous moment that only God could have conceived, the temptation of sexual sin in our own son's life, Brian and I paused at the intersection of Reconciliation Road.

In the calming glow of a yellowed sunrise light, Brian and I freely and openly forgave one another. The room filled with a peace that surpassed all our understanding. Brian shared his Spring Break experience of painting and packing, including a description of the reconciliation letter he had written me. In return, I shared my recent burial at the Buried Lies Cemetery. Not only did we agree to take a forward faith step to reconciliation, but we prayed together—praising the Lord for being our Healer, confessing our sinful choice to divorce, thanking Him for His grace, and asking Him to restore our broken family.

Post-divorce reconciliation is a poorly-paved path that few make the effort to drive. Our drive began by pursuing Christ's plan for reconciliation, first and foremost, through prayer and diving head first in to His Word. In addition, Brian and I read a resource recommended by our Divorce Care leaders titled *Reconcilable Differences*. The book, written by Jim Talley, "provides practical, biblical advice on how to resolve conflicts and develop a relationship based on mutual love, respect, and trust." Other than the Bible and a single Divorce Care session on the subject of reconciliation, Talley's book was the **only** resource we could find that came anywhere close to discussing reconciliation with the possibility of remarriage to your former spouse—a sad reality. In truth, much of our Reconciliation Road was paved in trust as we made a daily choice to forgive and move forward.

Just as Thomas had to see the markings on Christ's hands to believe in the truth of His resurrection, family and friends outside of our restored relationship were, for the most part, unsupportive and skeptical. Even our children had to see our healed scars to learn to trust again. We involved the children in every decision made, including our decision to remarry. Coincidentally (or God-incidentally), the day we closed the doors to our church plant was the day the Lord replanted our family tree. "A shoot will come up from the stump of Jesse; from his roots a Branch will bear fruit" (Isaiah 11:1-2).

On May 27, 2012, our family of five chose to "come up from the stump" and courageously say, "I do" all over again on the steps of the very church Brian and I were married at seventeen years before. Although it was against the will of many, it was completely in the will of God the Almighty. "And he has committed to us (the Smith 5) the ministry of reconciliation" (2 Corinthians 5:19). This January 7, 2014, Brian and I will celebrate twenty years of marriage (we choose to not count "the break") and ministry.

Sometimes I find myself asking, "Why us, Lord?" In the redundancy of the road trip, I hear Him hum, "Because you were willing. You did not choose me, but I chose and appointed you so that you might go and bear fruit—fruit that will last" (John 15:16). He is talking about fruit that will last on a road everlasting.

Reflections at the Well

Think about the "roads" you have traveled. What are some of the "historical markers" along the way?

What "step" in the forgiveness process is most challenging for you and why?

Who do you need to meet with at the intersection of Reconciliation Road?

End your time at the Well asking the Lord, through prayer, to bring to mind those you need to forgive as part of your restoration journey. Consider using the "steps" in the forgiveness process to forgive them.

Chapter 14

SUPERHEROES AMONG US

Instead, God chose things the world considers foolish in order to shame those who think they are wise. And he chose things that are powerless to shame those who are powerful. (1 Corinthians 1:27)

We have been living in a Pumpkin Patch—literally. One month ago, an eighteen-wheeler backed into an empty grass field on our church property to deliver several hundred pumpkins for our annual youth ministry Pumpkin Patch fundraiser. So, for thirty days our family of five, as well as a handful of church and community volunteers, have literally been "babysitting" (and selling) our little orange babies. Today is the last day of our Pumpkin Patch. Today is Halloween.

Now whether you are a fan of Halloween or not, you have to admit there is something empowering about assuming someone or something else's identity for an hour or two, especially when it involves the reward of candy. In full disclosure, my favorite costumes are superhero costumes. Talk about empowerment! There is nothing like slipping on those silver wristbands, a red bustier, blue power panties (yah, right) and a pair of tall red boots. Add a gold star-studded headband across your forehead and a looped lasso on your hip, and you have got yourself the perfect costume. Okay, I confess—I am a Wonder Woman fanatic.

Back in my day (at the risk of sounding like someone who is **way** past the age of wearing the afore-mentioned costume), there was such thing as "Underoos—the underwear that's fun to wear." I can still remember the sheer delight (and utter embarrassment), when my kindergarten "boy-friend" gave me my first and only pair of Wonder Woman "underoos" at my sixth birthday party. Wearing that top with those panties under any outfit was sure to produce superpowers that rivaled any actual superhero. When I wore this "armor" underneath, I felt empowered. I was invincible.

Maybe that is why, as human beings, we love the idea of superheroes—the idea that, no matter what may come our way, we are invincible. "Faster than a speeding bullet. More powerful than a locomotive. Able to leap tall buildings in a single bound. Look! Up in the sky! It's a bird. It's a plane. It's Superman!" Hardly ever do we consider the truth that, more often than not, superhe-

YOU AND I ARE SUPERHEROES.

roes are formed out of a broken and shameful past. They are not born superheroes. They become superheroes when they choose to use their "bad" for our "good."

You and I are superheroes. As we have journeyed away from our broken and shamed past and toward a loving and merciful God, we have learned useful tools and truths that can only be used for good. Not just for our good, but for the good of those around us. Simply put—God wastes no pain. What the devil meant for harm, can now be used for good. "You intended to harm me, but God intended it for good to accomplish what is now being done, the saving of many lives" (Genesis 50:20).

God Uses Imperfect People

According to Dr. Miriam Kinai, God uses imperfect and insignificant people to achieve His perfect and significant plans **if** they choose to cooperate with Him. He used Gideon (Judges 6-7), who was fearfully threshing wheat in a winepress, to lead an army of 300 to defeat Israel's enemies who were as numerous as locusts. This same Gideon said he was unqualified to save Israel because his clan was the weakest and he was the least important person in his father's house (talk about some self-esteem issues). But God already knew this when He chose Gideon to be Commander in Chief, and He promised to be with him.

Remember, when you are weak, He is strong. "My grace is sufficient for you, for my power is made perfect in weakness" (2 Corinthians 12:9). He will work on your weaknesses, as you faithfully work out your life's purpose. Believe me, I have served up many an excuse as to why I am not "qualified" to minister to shamed and broken women. At the writing of this book, I still have no Master's Degree in Divinity or Christian Counseling. All I have is some "street smarts," a real-life story to tell, and an all-powerful God to see that it is put to good use.

For some time, I believed the lie that I had to be perfect to preach His redemptive story. "Instead, God chose things the world considers foolish in order to shame those who think they are wise. And he chose things that are powerless to shame those who are powerful" (1 Corinthians 1:27). This is the kind of "shame" God endorses. Our stories of sexual shame to purposeful purity are stories that God can use to "shame" those who **think** they are "wise" (enough to keep on sinning). In other words, you do not have to be perfect to have purpose. In fact, I dare say that **if** we were perfect, the broken and shamed women of this world would not be willing to listen.

YOU DO NOT HAVE TO BE PERFECT TO HAVE PURPOSE.

I know it is scary to put it all "out there" (you are talking to someone who just spewed her sin to a potentially judgmental public over hundreds of pages). Gideon's fear did not flee overnight. He kept asking God for assurance, and God kept providing assurance through "heavenly hints." At some point and time, Gideon came in to agreement with God, and then his "superpowers" were unleashed.

Who can forget Moses? When Moses looked at his qualifications and current vocation as shepherd in a desert, He could not help but question God. "'Who am I, that I should go to Pharaoh and bring the Israelites out of Egypt?'" (Exodus 3:11). Moses also reminded God, the God who created him, that he was not an "eloquent" speaker. "The Lord said to him, 'Who gave man his mouth? Who makes him deaf or mute? Who gives him sight or makes him blind? Is it not I, the Lord? Now go; I will help you speak and will teach you what to say'" (Exodus 4:11-12). Do not disqualify yourself because of your "lack" of qualifications. God's presence in your life is all the qualifications you need to fulfill His purposes in your life.

What is the Lord asking of you? Who is He purposefully putting in your path? What ministry is He birthing in you? Decide now to use your "bad" for His "good." Empowering others was the final step in my restoration journey. To be honest, it was the most powerful step I took.

Empowering Others

At the risk of throwing out some Superman jargon, I believe the "kryptonite" in the lives of broken and shamed women can be summed up in two words—self and worth. Speaking from personal experience, these women are plagued with the poison of low self-esteem and self-worth. The strange thing is, more likely than not, these women are completely focused on self. One might even go so far as to say they are "selfish." Ouch, that hurts. I know this because I am one.

Currently, I own my own skincare and cosmetics business. My business is beauty. What is ironic about this (other than the fact that I am a total "tom boy" at heart), is I have always struggled with a poor self-image. My lack of self-worth, formed at my beginning, really messed with my head. I was always worried about what others thought of me. In a nutshell, it was all about me.

The moment I took the focus off of myself and put it on to others, my self-esteem grew. You could say that I found it empowering, just like a good pair of "Underoos." This was the same for my restoration journey. I remember the first time Brian and I were asked to share our reconciliation story during a message series at our church titled "Turnarounds." The series was built on biblical and real-life "turnaround" stories.

When the pastor asked us to share, I immediately said, "Yes!" Then, I freaked out. I was so nervous that I considered leaving my "adultery" portion of our testimony out even up to the point where we took the pulpit. That is, until I remembered God's promise to His children, "Whoever finds their life will lose it, and whoever loses their life for my sake will find it" (Matthew 10:39). In front of our entire congregation (which included our children), I confessed my adulterous affair. To my surprise, at the end of our testimony, we received a standing ovation. Following the service, women came up to me in tears thanking me for my honesty. "Your story has given me hope that I can be pure again," one young lady told me. It was then that I clearly heard God's call on my life.

Openly and honestly sharing my testimony, from adultery to purity, was and still is, empowering to me. But more than that, empowering others **through** my testimony is the most empowering act of all. In essence, we are empowered when we help others overcome. "And they overcame him by the blood of the Lamb, and by the word of their testimony" (Revelation 12:11).

Who can you help to overcome by the blood of the Lamb and the word of **your** testimony? What is the purpose behind your pain? I know now that God has a purpose for my pain and ultimate restoration—to use me to **reach** Christian women shamed by sexual sin and brokenness, **restore** them through relationship and resources, **replace** Satan's lies with God's truths, and then **release** them to reach broken women outside the church walls.

You and I have the opportunity to empower broken women through ministries in our own "backyard." If you live in fear because you grew up in an alcoholic home, why not empower women through your restoration story who also find themselves innocent victims of the disease? If you have been betrayed

THERE IS NOTHING MORE THERAPEUTIC THAN EMPOWERING OTHERS THROUGH OUR PAIN. GOD WASTES NO PAIN, INCLUDING YOURS.

by an unfaithful spouse, why not empower women through your restoration story who have also been betrayed? If you have experienced divorce, why not empower women through your restoration story who find themselves in the thick of divorce?

There is nothing more therapeutic than empowering others through our pain. God wastes no pain, including yours. For your final step on our restoration journey, I recommend finding a local ministry, or possibly starting your own, that lines up with your story. Search the internet or phone book for the ministries that match you. Two local ministries that are near and dear to my heart are Jesus Said Love and Restore Her.

Jesus Said Love

Jesus Said Love (or JSL) exists to share the revolutionary love of Christ toward women in the sex industry. They **go** into strip clubs monthly, **love** dancers where they are, and **connect** them to various community resources and local churches. www.jesussaidlove.com

Restore Her

Restore Her rescues girls who have been exposed to commercial or private sexual exploitation. Texas leads the nation as a hub for human trafficking and *Restore Her* is committed to lead the nation in not only rescuing these victims, but seeing their lives change through a quality, Christian education. www.restoreher.org

Your story is not for you, it is meant for someone else. Do not let your life pass without sharing your restoration story with someone else. They need to hear it, and you need to share it. "Wonder Woman, Wonder Woman. Now the world is ready for you, and the wonders you can do." What can God do through you? There is only one way to find out.

Reflections at the Well

Who is your favorite superhero and why? How are you similar?

God uses imperfect and insignificant people to achieve His perfect and significant plans **if** they choose to cooperate with Him. How are you cooperating or not cooperating with God?

Who can you help to overcome by the blood of the Lamb and the word of **your** testimony? What is the purpose behind your pain?

End your time at the Well researching local ministries where you could use your "bad" for "good." If you are unable to find a ministry, consider, through the Lord's leading, "birthing" a ministry of your own. Ask the Lord, what are you birthing in me?

Chapter 15

FROM SHAME TO HONOR

Anyone who believes in him will never be put to shame. (Romans 10:11)

Recently, like most Americans, I was glued to the TV for the 2014 mid-term elections. Do not worry. I am not going to go all "political" on you. One by one, the losing candidates stood with hidden humiliation before a room of their constituents (not to mention a TV audience of millions), gracefully accepting the agony of their defeat. In vast contrast, the winners stood with honor, before their constituents and the exact same TV audience, to proudly deliver their acceptance speeches. In every election, there are winners and losers—honor and shame.

Reminds me of a game I used to play growing up. You might be familiar with it. It was a little game they called "Red Rover." One by one, children were called by the opposing team to run, with all their might, the length of the school playground in an attempt to "break through" the opposing team's hand-in-hand wall. If you could break through the wall, you were free to return to your original team with someone from the opposing team in tow. The strong would strut back to their wall with honor. In vast contrast, if you could not break through the wall, you immediately became a "prisoner" of the opposing team, shamefully taking your place along the wall of losers. In the end, the team with the most players left wins.

For Red Rover strategy purposes, the weak ones were always called first. I was always called first. As if that was not shameful enough, try hobbling across the playground with stiff leg braces. Because I was pigeon-toed, I wore "special shoes" that connected to metal bars that ran the length of my body that fastened to an ugly Velcro "belt" around my waist. Yes, I wore "magic shoes" before Forest Gump made them cool. "Run, Traci! Run!" In my humble opinion, "Rover" was "Red" because of the humiliated red faces of the "weaker" kids.

Although this "fun" tradition caused me great trauma and angst in my impressionable childhood years, it was nothing compared to the utter shame and humiliation Christ endured on the cross:

Wanting to satisfy the crowd, Pilate released Barabbas to them. He had Jesus flogged, and handed him over to be crucified. The soldiers led Jesus away into the palace (that is, the Praetorium) and called together the whole company of soldiers. They put a purple robe on him, then twisted together a crown of thorns and set it on him. And they began to call out to him, 'Hail, king of the Jews!' Again and again they struck him on the head with a staff and spit on him. And when they had mocked him, they took off the purple robe and put his own clothes on him. Then they led him out to crucify him. A certain man from Cyrene, Simon, the father of Alexander and Rufus, was passing by on his way in from the country, and they forced him to carry the cross. They brought Jesus to the place called Golgotha (which means The Place of the Skull). Then they offered him wine mixed with myrrh, but he did not take it. And they crucified him. Dividing up his clothes, they cast lots to see what each would get. (Mark 15:15-24)

Have you ever stopped to consider why Christ's crucifixion was so public? If it was only necessary for Jesus to die for our sins, He could have been executed privately. But public mocking and humiliation, according to the Scriptures, was vital to the redemptive work of the crucifixion. In fact, prophets predicted that public humiliation and mocking would accompany the work of the Messiah:

"I offered my back to those who beat me, my cheeks to those who pulled out my beard; I did not hide my face from mocking and spitting" (Isaiah 50:6).

"Marshall your troops, O city of troops, for a siege is laid against us. They will strike Israel's ruler on the cheek with a rod" (Micah 5:1).

"But I am a worm and not a man, scorned by men and despised by the people. All who see me mock me; they hurl insults, shaking their heads: 'He trusts in the Lord; let the Lord rescue him. Let him deliver him, since he delights in him" (Psalm 22:6-8).

"I am poured out like water, and all my bones are out of joint. My heart has turned to wax; it has melted away within me. My strength is dried up like a potsherd, and my tongue sticks to the roof of my mouth; you lay me in the dust of death. Dogs have surrounded me; a band of evil men has encircled me, they have pierced my hands and feet. I can count all my bones; people stare and gloat over me. They divide my garments among them and cast lots for my clothing" (Psalm 22:14-18).

"You know that I am scorned, disgraced and shamed; all my enemies are before you. Scorn has broken my heart and has left me helpless; I looked for sympathy, but there was none, for comforters, but I found none. They put gall in my food and gave me vinegar for my thirst" (Psalm 69:19-21).

To fully understand the necessity for humiliation, it is important to understand the difference between shame and honor. The people of ancient societies, who incidentally wrote the books in the Bible, lived in a shame verses honor world. Honor was equivalent to a good reputation, esteem, and respect. To honor someone was to recognize the value of that person and act accordingly. In an honor-based society, you had no worth unless others gave it to you. Reputation was everything.

In contrast, shame was synonymous with humiliation and loss of standing. To shame someone was to challenge that person's reputation or disregard their worth. Shame was used as a substitute for nakedness. The punishments inflicted on Jesus, like the flogging and crucifixion, were not just physically gruesome. Their purpose was to shame—render someone helpless, naked, and publicly exposed.

I have a really cool friend from church. She is not only cool because she loves the Lord, but she is an academia author and History professor at Texas A&M University (one of the finest institutes in these great states called America. Okay, I am partial). We like to meet for lunch on occasion at this "cool" sushi place in town to discuss all things history and theology. Believe me, it is cool to have lunch with a published author and professor.

When my friend found out I was writing this book, she was very intrigued. In fact, she had just taught a class at our church about the very subject of shame verses honor (much of which I have used as a resource for this chapter). To prepare for her presentation, she researched the history of shame and honor in the United States. During the American Revolution and up to 1861, privates in the U.S. Army could be flogged, but officers could not. Because officers were supposed to be gentleman and men of social standing, public reputations were everything. Flogging a gentleman was so shameful that it would destroy their very worth in a way in which they could never fully recover. It was considered worse than killing them.

According to my friend, the professor, ancients viewed every human action and interaction as an occasion for either gaining honor (increasing one's value in the public eye) or for being shamed (having one's estimation degraded). The desire to maintain honor was a powerful incentive for right action.

Flashback to Chapter 1 and the original sin committed in the Garden of Eden. "The man and his wife were both naked, and they felt no shame." At this moment, Adam and Eve's honor was still intact. But as soon as they took a bite out of that big **red** apple, their honor turned to shame because God went public with their sin.

GOD ACTS TOWARD US, NOT ONLY OUT OF HIS UNCONDITIONAL LOVE FOR US, BUT MORE IMPORTANTLY, OUT OF HIS HONOR.

God's own honor is very important to Him. It is so important that God's Name is spelled with a capital "N" throughout the Bible. His Name is His fame, His reputation, and His honor. God acts toward us, not only out of His unconditional love for us, but more importantly, out of His honor. "For the sake of His great Name the Lord will not reject his people because the Lord was pleased to make you his own" (1 Samuel 12:22). The fact that God is jealous of His honor makes His willingness to be shamed for our sake an act of incredible love.

So how does all of this apply to us as broken and shamed women? Our sin shames us, especially when it goes public. More times than not, this sin causes us to suffer public humiliation and rejection. The rejection of others causes us to question our own self-worth. In our minds, we think, "It is just better to keep my sin a secret." But even when our sin remains secret and unexposed to the public, God still exposes our sin to us, not to shame us, but rather, to restore us. "He will bring to light what is hidden in darkness and will expose the motives of men's hearts" (1 Corinthians 4:5).

The Lord brought to light what was hidden in my life, the shame that began as a little girl, so that I could ultimately be restored. Just as the consequences of sin should be death, the consequences of sin exposed should be shame. But shame was never meant to be a part of my story. Shame was never meant to be a part of your story either. Praise the Lord that through one sacrificial act, Jesus' suffering a shame-filled death on the cross, you and I are set free from shame forever.

Instead of shame, God gives us honor. In fact, He has promised that through Jesus' shame, we will never be put to shame. "If you declare with your mouth, 'Jesus is Lord,' and believe in your heart that God raised him from the dead, you

INSTEAD OF SHAME, GOD GIVES US HONOR.

will be saved. For it is with your heart that you believe and are justified, and it is with your mouth that you profess your faith and are saved. As Scripture says, 'Anyone who believes in him will never be put to shame'" (Romans 10:9-11). Notice this scripture says "anyone"—even a broken and shamed woman at the well.

Reflections at the Well

According to ancient times, what is the difference between shame and honor?

Why was it necessary for Christ's crucifixion to be so shameful and public?

How does Christ's shame restore honor to us?

End your time at the Well thanking the Lord for your restored honor.

Final Words

MOVING FORWARD RESTORED

But who are you, O man, to talk back to God? Shall what is formed say to him who formed it, 'Why did you make me like this?' Does not the potter have the right to make out of the same lump of clay some pottery for noble purposes and some for common use? (Romans 9:20-21)

I knew this day was coming—the day that you and I would reach the end of our restoration journey together. To be honest, I am a little emotional, but in a good way. Call me nostalgic, but I thought it only fitting that I write these final words from my favorite local coffee-clad writing venue—Mugwalls. You would not believe the changes here.

The walls, once decorated with dirtied and cracked coffee mugs, are now "mug-less." Fresh paint. Fresh furnishings. Fresh faces. Mugwalls is different, but in a good way.

Oh, how I wish you were sitting across this rickety table from me—I can only imagine the changes in you. What was once dirty in you is now deemed a child of God. What was once stained in you is now saved to save others. What was once used in you is now useful for God's purposes.

You have faithfully finished this journey, and now the Lord is calling you to more.

The Lord says to you as he said to me,

Therefore, I am now going to allure her; I will lead her into the wilderness and speak tenderly to her. There I will give her back her vineyards, and will make the Valley of Achor a door of hope. There she will respond as in the days of her youth, as in the day she came up out of Egypt. "In that day," declares the Lord, you will call me 'my husband'; you will no longer call me 'my master.'" (Hosea 2:14-16)

He is leading you into the wilderness to speak tenderly to you. He will continue to restore your vineyards, and will use your brokenness as a vessel of hope to others. Through His gracious love and mercy, He will call you His unblemished bride forever.

Broken by sin. Restored by Him. You and I are beautifully broken.

CPSIA information can be obtained
at www.ICGtesting.com
Printed in the USA
FSOW01n0159030215
4970FS